T0150893

THE
SECRET TO
ACHIEVING
ALL YOUR GOALS

THE
SECRET TO
ACHIEVING
ALL YOUR GOALS

An Advanced Course in
Personal Achievement

Roger Dawson

MEDIA

Published 2019 by Gildan Media LLC
aka G&D Media
www.GandDmedia.com

FIRST EDITION 2019

Front Cover design by David Rheinhardt of Pyrographx

Interior design by Meghan Day Healey of Story Horse, LLC

Library of Congress Cataloging-in-Publication Data is available upon request

ISBN: 978-1-7225-0027-6

10   9   8   7   6   5   4   3   2   1

Contents

Chapter One

Learning to Go Beyond Goal Setting and Positive Thinking

O nce upon a time, in a beautiful old gold rush town in the Rocky Mountains of Canada called Opportunity, there lived a flock of long necked geese. On a beautiful fall morning when the surrounding mountains were glowing with the bright red and yellows of the fall scenery, it was time for the geese to take off for their annual migration to their winter feeding grounds in Mexico. As was the custom, this was a big day for the townspeople of Opportunity, the day when they all came out to see the geese leave. As if programmed to do so, the geese took off with a great flapping of wings. They circled the lake twice and then headed south to the cheers of the townspeople.

Several days later, the geese were approaching Contentment, Colorado, a town that Quaker pilgrims founded in 1857. They saw a beautiful lake on the outskirts of town, and decided to spend the night there. It was the most beautiful lake they'd ever seen, and the next day they decided to stay for another night. There was plenty of food for them to eat, and they were very happy there. Two days turned into a week, and nobody wanted to leave except one or two of the younger geese who went to their leaders and said, "Winter is coming to Contentment, and we must leave this beautiful place soon, and fly on to Mexico. The only way we'll get back to Opportunity in the spring, is if we leave Contentment now."

However, most of the geese were happy there, and wanted to stay longer. "Why take the risk and make the effort to fly on, when things may be much worse further south? Everything we need is right here."

Several weeks passed, the first winter storm blew in, and the lake started to freeze. Soon the geese had trouble finding enough food, and began to grow weak. The kindly Quakers who lived in the town felt sorry for the geese, and started to feed them. After a while the geese gathered at the side of the lake every morning waiting for the townspeople to give them food.

The geese weren't lazy. Every day they flew around in circles, went to endless meetings with the other geese, and spent many hours rearranging their homes at the edge of the lake. They were always busy—but they quit looking for food, because they knew the townspeople would always take care of them.

One day a stranger was traveling through town, and stopped to watch the townspeople feeding the geese. "Why are you spending so much of your time and money feeding the geese," he asked. "You're poor people, and winter is coming. You should be worrying about your own survival. Besides, geese are wild birds and they should learn to feed themselves."

The townspeople didn't want to appear stupid to the stranger, so they quickly made up a reason for feeding the geese. "Why stranger, can't you see that we're fattening these geese up for our Christmas dinner? This year we will have the greatest feast that we have ever had."

And that's what happened. The townspeople all had a wonderful Christmas dinner, and the geese never made it to Mexico. They all perished in Contentment. The moral of the story is that if you get stuck in contentment, somebody's going to wring your neck and cook your goose!

Doesn't that fable represent the lives of so many people? We start with such great ambition, determined that nothing will stand in the way of us accomplishing our goals. And in this great land of opportunity, if we study and work hard, we have an excellent chance of becoming successful—we will achieve our goals. This could be the worst thing that will ever happen to us. Because when we achieve our goals, we often arrive at the land of contentment and never realize that if we were to take off and fly again, we could achieve so much more. As George Bernard Shaw said: "There are two tragedies in life. One is not getting your heart's desire. The other is to get it."

I believe that *it is a virtue to be content with what we have—but it is a vice to be content with what we are.* Too many people congeal at some point in their lives. They reach a point where they don't want to change any more. They become content with what they have become, and their belief about their potential congeals like cooking fat getting cold in the bottom of a frying pan. A human mind is a terrible thing to waste. It's even more tragic when the mind is one that was successful in the past, but is now congealing in contentment.

In this book I will not only make you want to take off and fly again, but what is more important, I will show you *how* to do it.

There are many fine audio programs in my library that stress how important it is to set goals and maintain a positive attitude. Playing them in my car over the last 30 years has kept me going through some tough times. I credit them for much of my success, as do hundreds of thousands of other listeners throughout the country and around the world.

The key phrases I can quote word for word because I've listened to them dozens of times.

Earl Nightingale said: *"You become what you think about."*

Napoleon Hill declared: *"Whatever the mind of man can conceive and believe, it can achieve."*

Robert Schuller proclaimed: *"When faced with a mountain, I will not quit! I will keep on striving until I climb over, find a pass through, tunnel underneath or simply stay and turn the mountain into a gold mine, with God's help."*

I still have the phonograph record that made Earl Nightingale famous. A friend gave me a copy of *The Strangest Secret* in 1967, and in only thirty days, it turned my life from failure to success.

All of these positive-thinking messages hinge on one idea: that if you can change the way you think, you can change your future. Karl Menninger, the famous psychiatrist from Topeka, Kansas, said that what happens to you doesn't matter. It's how you react to what happens to you that makes the difference. William James, who became known as the father of American psychology, said that the most important discovery of his generation was that a man could change his circumstances by changing the way he thinks.

None of this is new. The Greek philosopher Epictetus said, "People are disturbed not by things, but by the view that they take of them." In Hamlet, a play with enough delicious sound bites to make a modern politician green with envy, Hamlet said, "There's nothing either good or bad but thinking makes it so."

I agree with all of this, but the purpose of this book is to take you beyond goal setting and positive thinking. After you've learned to set goals, write them down and carry them around with you, after you've learned to act as though it's impossible to fail, if you're still not where you want to be, then what do you do? If you're already very successful, but still have a feeling that you could do even more if only someone would show you the way, to whom do you turn? How do you go beyond all that?

I firmly believe that we can all do so much more than we think we can do. I used to run a company for a man who was always telling me that. I would complain to him that he was asking me to push our employees too hard, and he would say, "Roger, everybody can do so much more than they think they can do. The only way you'll ever get the best out of people is to push them too hard."

I'd like to challenge you with that statement. I think you can do far more than you think you can do. Doesn't that ring true when you think about it? Aren't you doing far more now than you thought you could do five years ago? I believe that five years from now, you can be doing far more than you dream is possible today. The only way you'll ever get the best out of yourself is to push yourself too hard, too soon. Always attempt a little more than you think you're capable of doing, and always move to the next challenge just a little ahead of when you think you're ready.

Congratulations on achieving all your goals so far, but I want to see you achieve greater success than you presently think is possible. I promise you that I'll do more than just stand on the sideline, to be the coach who cheers you on. This is not a motivational program; it's a skill building program. I'm going to teach you the skills that are necessary for you to become all that you're capable of becoming.

Everything that I have to teach you in this program I've based on one premise—that in order for things to change in your life, your behavior has to change. Changing the way you think is fine, but it only helps you get what you want out of life, if it leads to a change in behavior. So in this program, I'm going to teach you how to change what you're doing, in order to change where you're going. And since you can't soar beyond your potential without the help of others, I'm also going to give you the power to change the behavior of the other people in your life.

Let's look at what you'll learn from this book, so that you get a feel for what it can do for you.

For the balance of chapter one, I'll teach you what controls your future and what you can do to change your direction. I'll teach you the difference between cognitive psychology that tells you to change your thinking if you want to change your behavior; and *behavior shaping*, which tells you first to change your behavior. And then changing your behavior will automatically change the way you think.

In chapter two you'll learn the four drives that control your behavior and how to identify your dominant driving force. Once you understand this you'll know why you do the things you do.

In chapter three I'll teach you some remarkable research on exactly how to modify your thinking so that you always behave in an upbeat, optimistic way despite any discouragement that tries to drag you down.

In chapters four, five and six, I'll take you into the heart of this program: the latest research on behavior shaping, and how to use it to change your own behavior and that of everybody with whom you deal. It's a method that will greatly shorten your learning curve, and dramatically cut the time it takes you to influence other people. I'll teach you about a dramatic breakthrough in behavior shaping developed by Pat and Marty Roberts. I didn't believe their claims until I saw their method in action, and it will astonish you also.

In many cases, the way we train people is not only incredibly inefficient but often it's all wrong. I believe that techniques in management and sales that we've taken for granted for years are taking us away from what we're trying to accomplish. You'll see how learning the fundamentals of behavior shaping will dramatically affect your ability to motivate yourself and other people. You'll learn how to identify existing reinforcers, and to rearrange those reinforcers to link them to the desired behavior change.

In chapter seven I'll teach you how to use behavior shaping to eradicate your fears. In chapters eight and nine I'll teach you eight ways to use behavior shaping to change other people's behavior—how to get people on your team.

Then in chapter ten you'll meet Dan Hill, a mid-level executive whose career is in a rut. He's the sales manager for a division of a large corporation. While he's done well in the past, his career is stalled and he doesn't know how to get it moving again. You'll learn how he uses the techniques in this program to try to move up in his corporation. You'll be with him every step of the way until he's finally called into the world headquarters of his corporation in New York, to hear what they have planned for him.

That's a quick look at where we're going together. All the new things I have to share with you have me so excited, that I can't wait to get started! Get ready to enjoy *The Secret to Achieving All Your Goals: An Advanced Course in Personal Achievement.*

Psychologists line up in three camps when it comes to helping their patients achieve more.

First are the people in the cognitive camp, who concentrate on thinking, imaging, emotions and feelings. Cognitive therapists believe that the way you think is the key to the way you behave. That to change your future you must first change the way you *think,* and that will lead to a change in behavior.

Second are the people in the behavioral camp, who concentrate on what people do, rather than why they do it. Behavioral therapists believe that our past has conditioned us to behave the way we do, and the way we *behave* causes us to think the way we do.

In the third camp are the metaphysicians— most people know them as positive thinkers—who believe that thought alone controls your future. I'm not knocking positive thinking. There have been times in my life when a shot of it was just what I needed. However, O J Simpson is a positive thinker, and he's doing 33 years in a Nevada prison. Bernie Madoff was a positive thinker, and he's serving a 150-year sentence. If you motivate someone who's going in the wrong direction, you'll help him or her get there faster—but they'll still show up in the wrong place!

Those are the choices you have. The cognitive camp, telling you to change the way you think; the behavioral camp telling you to change what you're doing; and the motivators telling you that there is not a thing wrong with you and that there's nothing you can't do.

The philosophy of any one of these groups will help you achieve your goals, but if you want to achieve your full potential, you must decide which one is right for you. Imagine that you're racing off down the road to success. At first, it's like the start of the New York Marathon. Tens of thousands of people are on the same road, racing for the same prize. Soon most of the others fall behind, and you're out in front with just a few hundred people. Suddenly the road to success forks into three branches. The people ahead of you are all going off in all three directions. Consider the options. Whom do you want to follow?

Off to the right are the positive thinkers and metaphysicians. They believe that all you have to do is think about your goal and it will happen. It's tempting to follow the positive thinkers as they skip off into the sunset. It looks like the easiest way, and they do seem happy. By the way, have you ever seen a metaphysicians map? It has "You are here," written all over it! These positive thinkers are talking excitedly about a study done with basketball players, which they claim proves that you don't have to practice shooting baskets to get better. You can lie down and just think about doing it and get the same effect.

Wouldn't it be wonderful if that were true? Perhaps if we wanted to become President of the United States, all we'd have to do would be to lie down and think about it, and soon the Marine band would show up at our door playing "Hail to the Chief." Sure beats kissing all those babies!

To me this kind of thinking is an extension of the unrealistic goals that we often have when we're young. Ask your fifteen-year-old son what he wants to become, and he might say, "I'm going to become a world famous rock musician like Ozzy Osborne."

So you say, "But you don't know how to play a guitar."

"Yeah, I know, but that's not going to stop me."

"But you don't even know how to read music."

"Neither does Ozzy Osborne. Dad, you're so out of touch. You don't have to know any of that stuff to be a rock musician." That's the equivalent of saying, "Flap my wings and fly down to Mexico for the winter? No problem!"

The problem with young ambition is that it hasn't learned the law of cause and effect. You can't just imagine yourself becoming a world famous musician and expect it to happen just because you want it so much. When Earl Nightingale said, "You become what you think about," he didn't mean that's *all* you have to do. Trust me on that! I knew Earl Nightingale. Earl Nightingale was a friend of mine. He meant that thinking in that manner would create a new self-image, which would then cause you *to do the things you had to do, to get you where you want to go.*

As we go into our twenties, we learn the law of cause and effect. If we really want to be President, we must devote a lifetime to learning how to play politics. Then we must shake thousands of hands and raise millions of dollars. Lyndon Johnson even had that down to a science. "Every hand I shake is worth 150 votes," he would say. "Because they'll all tell other people what a great guy I was to shake their hand, and then they'll tell even more people." As we get older, we learn that if we want to lose weight, we have to quit drinking alcohol, eat less and exercise more, not expect a miracle. That if we want to become rich, we have to become a better person: more skilled, more persistent, more motivated.

So we're tempted to follow the positive thinkers and metaphysicians because it does seem like a short cut to success—but we have an uneasy feeling that it may be too good to be true.

Next we watch the cognitive thinkers going off on the road to the left, to see if what they're saying makes sense. They say that it isn't as simple as the metaphysicians and positive thinkers would have you believe. That changing the way you think will change the way you behave, and that's what makes you successful. How would that relate to shooting baskets? It means that if you believed you could become a good basketball player, you'd want to try shooting some baskets and see if you were any good at it. Then if you found that you were terrible, you'd be in control of your thoughts enough to persist until you did get good. That makes more sense. Changing the way you think probably would lead to changing the way you behave.

However there's a third branch on the road to success and I want us to go down it together. It's the way taken by behavior shapers, who say that if you change your behavior even the smallest amount, and reward that change, it will lead to improved performance, and that is what changes your thinking. Behavior shapers say that if you want to get good at shooting baskets or anything else, start doing it in a supportive environment and keep on doing it until you become a master at it. *If something is worth doing, it's worth doing poorly until you get good at it.*

Johnny Ace Palmer, the world champion magician, is a close friend of mine. The World Conference of Magicians voted him world champion at their convention in Holland. Not only that, he was also the first close-up magician ever to receive the award. To watch him perform makes me marvel that anybody can be as good at anything as he is with sleight of hand magic. He can make a Coke bottle appear out of thin air. He can wave his hand and make anything disappear. When he appears at the Magic Castle in Hollywood, he gets standing ovations from his peers. Once we flew back from Chicago together after filming a television show. We talked for a while and then I said, "Want to play some cards?"

He looked at me in astonishment, and said, "I don't normally play cards, Roger."

"Why not?" I asked him.

"Because it wouldn't be fair."

"Oh, come on," I said. "Let's play some poker."

"OK, but I won't bet with you," he told me. I asked the flight attendant for a deck of cards. He unwrapped them and then started shuffling. I thought that he was taking longer than normal to shuffle, but apart from that, I didn't notice anything unusual. Then he dealt our hands and turned his over. He had dealt himself a straight flush.

I said, "OK! I think that's enough cards. What do you want to do next?"

Johnny stopped by the house recently and I shared with him my feeling that people today are too concerned with what they think, and not concerned enough about what they do. "I couldn't agree with you more, Roger," he told me. "Let me show you a trick that will illustrate the point you're making." He pulled a penny and a half-dollar out of his pocket, and laid them in the palm of his hand. Suddenly the half-dollar disappeared. Then he tossed the penny up in the air, and in midair it seemed to change into a half-dollar. He tossed the half-dollar up and it changed back into a penny. I was sitting only a foot away, and had no idea how he was doing it. "That's unbelievable, Johnny. How long did it take you to learn how to do that?"

"About four years," he told me. I was dying to ask him how he did it, but I know he won't tell me, so I never ask.

To my surprise he said, "I'm going to break a rule, and show you how I do it. It's the only way I can make my point. What I'm doing is back palming the other coin. Back palm is an expression that we magicians use to describe holding the coin between our fingers on the back of our hands." He turned his hand over so that the palm was down, and showed me how he was gripping the edge of the coin between the back of his fingers. "When it appears to disappear I've really moved it to back palm, so that I'm gripping the edge of it between the back of my fingers. When I appear to be tossing the penny up in the air, I'm really throwing the half-dollar from the back of my hand. As I toss it, I move the penny in my palm to my back palm."

"So it's really a very simple trick?" I asked him.

"It's simple, but it takes extraordinary skill. There are only four other people in the world that can do what I've just shown you. It takes incredible manual dexterity, so you need to warm up your fingers to do it, the way that a concert pianist warms up. The problem is that magicians don't get a chance to warm up. We have to move into an illusion like this and get it right the first time. If I could warm up first, I could have learned to do this in only one year. To be able to do it on command took me four years. So, here's how this relates to what you were saying about thinking as opposed to doing. When I was learning to do this, I tried to visualize the penny changing into the half-dollar. For hours, I would sit there tossing the coins up, trying to visualize them changing. It didn't help. What I found out was that if I wanted to learn how to do this, I had to be willing to do it badly, and then keep working at it until I could do it poorly. After six months, I could do it adequately, but not well enough to do it in public. Only after a year of practice could I do it without effort. To do it on command took me three more years of practice."

What Johnny Ace Palmer was telling me about magic applies to anything else you want to accomplish in life. Positive thinking is wonderful, but only if it leads to a change in behavior. To do something well, you must do it badly until you can do it poorly, and poorly until you can do it adequately, and then keep honing your skill until you can do it well. As I said before, *if something is worth doing, it's worth doing poorly until you get good at it.*

While cognitive psychologists and behavior shapers differ widely on how to become successful, they both agree on one thing. That for things to change in your life, one way or another your *behavior* has to change. And you know what? It's a lot easier to change the way you behave than to change the way you think. Would you give me an amen on that? Of course you would!

Look at what you're doing right now. You're reading this book, which tells me that you're an intelligent, disciplined person, who's willing to make an investment in your future. So your behavior is—you're reading this book. Your thoughts however, may be somewhere else. You may be thinking, "Self improvement is hard work. I put in a good day's work, so perhaps I'll relax now and get back to this book later." You're tempted to stop reading and turn on the television. That would be a new behavior. You could pay a therapist a thousand dollars to find out why you have a tendency to start doing something, and then quit before you see things through. The therapist would probably do a great job of teaching you why you think the way you do. He or she may even be able to change the way you think. However, you have another choice. The other choice you have is simply to change the way you behave: don't quit reading this book. Just keep on reading! Isn't that an incredible shortcut?

I'm not even sure that understanding why you do counter-productive things is going to help you anyway. Albert Ellis, the brilliant founder of the rational-emotive school of therapy, says this: "Insight will help you very little. (You think that) your knowledge of how you got disturbed will make you less neurotic? Drivel! It will often make you nuttier!" Albert Ellis is my kind of person!

By now, you know that I believe that *what you do* is far more germane to your success than how you think. If you feel that you're capable of achieving more than you've done so far, it's a good bet that your behavior stands between you and where you want to go. In short, you're doing something wrong! The question is: why do you do things that are clearly not in your best interests? Why do you fail to do the things that would make your life easier, richer, and more fun? I will answer those questions, and give you the tools you need to start doing the things you need to do to reach your full potential. At the same time, you'll learn how to eliminate self-destructive behavior. Not only your own—you'll be able also to influence other people's behavior using the same techniques.

This is above all a practical book. I think that people look at their performance with an overemphasis on the deep psychological forces that they imagine are at work, and an *under emphasis* on behavior. Success is nothing more than an interaction between what you do, where you do it, and how you reinforce that behavior.

There's no question that William James was right when he said that you could change your circumstances by changing the way you think. Remember, however, that changing your attitude doesn't get you anywhere unless it leads to a change in behavior. Somewhere down the line thoughts have to turn into actions. So, the real purpose of changing the way you think is that a change in thinking leads to a change in behavior. In this book, I'm going to explore with you a sensational shortcut: how about simply changing your behavior and skip having to change the way you think first? And you know what? As I'll prove to you before we're through, changing your behavior is a lot easier than changing the way you think!

Next I want to teach you the AC/DC formula. Everybody has one of four driving forces, and I'm going to analyze yours for you, so you can begin to understand why you behave the way you do.

Chapter Two

Know Your Driving Life Force

In this chapter, I am going to lay the groundwork for everything that follows by teaching you which of the four driving life forces dominates your behavior.

When you're very young one of these driving forces rises up inside you and influences everything you do for the rest of your life. When you learn which one is your driving life force, you'll know why you behave the way you do. Then when you learn to attune your energy to your driving life force, you'll be amazed at the quantum leaps in achievement you'll take.

Let's start out with a little goal setting. Before you start out on a journey, it's a good idea to find out if you really want to go there. I want you to take a leap in faith and assume that if you apply the techniques in this program they will give you anything you want. I also want you to imagine that whatever you decide to go for, you will never run out of money, and your health will stay good. With all of these assurances, I want you to answer the following questions. They will give you a tremendous insight into your driving life force.

Would you rather be poor but famous like Mother Theresa, or rich and unknown like billionaire Daniel K. Ludwig? Would you rather be Jimmy Fallon, the host of the Tonight Show, who must constantly prove himself; or Jacques Cousteau who can ride on his reputation? Would you rather own your own company that earned you a million dollars a year, or be president of a huge corporation with a salary of a million dollars a year? Would you rather be a famous golfer whom everyone loves; or a famous surgeon whom few people know but who helps save people's lives?

Would you rather be a U.S. Senator from a large state such as California, or the governor of a small state like Delaware?

If you'll analyze why you answered the way you did, it will tell you a great deal about what's important to you in life. Most of us can answer these questions without thinking. We know very clearly what appeals to us. However, few of us know *why* things are important to us. I have developed what I call the AC/DC formula. Once I've explained it to you, and given you some examples, you'll know why some things are meaningful to you, and some things are not.

The four life forces that drive our behavior are AC/DC: Acceptance, Control, Direction and Competence, and one of these will dominate everything you do in life. If you've been working hard, but not getting very far, probably you have been resisting your life force. Which means that you think what you've been doing is important to you, but deep down inside, it is empty and meaningless. To make quantum leaps in your success, you must attune what you're doing to your driving life force. Then you'll see how success will flow to you.

Knowing the life force that drives your behavior is a major key to going to a new level of achievement, so let's look at each of the four separately.

Acceptance

If your driving life force is acceptance, the most important thing in life to you is earning the acceptance of others. Children all go through a phase when this is foremost in their minds, because parents and teachers have trained them to respond to this. For children who are four, five and six, nothing is more important to them than being liked by their parents and teachers. When they're seven, eight and nine, nothing beats being liked and accepted by their friends. Then, in their teenage years they often rebel against this and become very individualistic in their style. This can be radical, as in the teenager who wears earrings in his nose, and dies his hair purple. Or it can be subtler, as in the case of a doctor's daughter who enrolls in medical school but deliberately fails as rebellion against merely following her father's will. So, to a greater or lesser extent, in one way or another, most of us outgrow our need for acceptance. However some people never outgrow it and it becomes the dominant driving force in their lives.

Former President Jimmy Carter would be a good example of an Acceptance person. Much of his popularity came from being liked rather than being admired. He over-reacted to polls and shied away from doing things he should have done for fear that people wouldn't like him for it. This probably came from having a domineering father and a strict mother. When he was in the middle of his first term as governor of Georgia, he came home to the family farm, sat down in his mother's bedroom, and put his feet up on her bed. "I'm thinking of running for President," he told her.

"President of what?" she said, genuinely confused.

"President of the United States, and I'm going to win," he told her.

She snorted and told him, "Take your feet off my bed."

As we'll see, children who don't feel love and security in their early years will grow up to be Acceptance people.

Control

The second major drive is Control. An obvious example of a control person would be a dictator: an Adolf Hitler or a Joseph Stalin—the little man who wants to fight back. However, it can be subtler than that: schoolteachers, nurses, and psychologists may all be driven by the enjoyment of controlling other people. I've always thought that a top salesperson, the one who has the killer instinct to make a sale, is a control freak. His burning desire to influence people is easy to spot: if he's not selling his product or service, he'll have a pocketful of lottery tickets to unload. When he's not trying to get money from somebody, he'll be persuading them to buy the same make of car as he drives, or live the same part of town. In my mind, the strong turn-on he gets from influencing people is just control dominance in disguise.

However, control over other people is only a small part of the picture, because control people also want to be in command of all other areas in their lives. This person won't go to a party unless they know who is going to be there, and is so organized that they know exactly where everything is.

Richard Nixon is a good example of a control person. Remember how frustrated he got when he couldn't control the press? When he lost the California gubernatorial race in 1962 he told them, "You won't have Nixon to push around anymore because, gentlemen, this is my last press conference." After Watergate, you would think that he'd have gone into hibernation, but it wasn't long before he was back knocking on the White House door, trying to persuade the current President to his point of view.

Nixon's father was a bitter, violent and unpleasant man, and because he was one of five children, he got little love from his mother. However, he was born, raised and went to college in a small community where everyone knew him. Control people are usually raised in a secure environment with little love.

Direction

The third major drive in my AC/DC formula is Direction. Very early in life Direction people develop a very stubborn philosophy, and it's unlikely that anything will ever budge them from their beliefs. To them, being right is more important than being loved or respected. What many would criticize as excessive ambition is often a strong sense of direction in disguise. A priest or a minister would be a good example of this, but many successful people develop convictions early in life. If one day *Sixty Minutes* interviews your kindergarten teacher, and she says about you, "Oh, yes, even way back then you could tell that he would become rich one day," you'll know you're a direction freak!

Former President Ronald Reagan would be a good example of a Direction controlled person. I have followed his career from when he first ran for governor of California, and it always seemed to me that the jobs he held as governor and President were less important than the conservative message in which he believed. The jobs just happened to be in the path of the direction in which he was going.

Reagan's father was an alcoholic who couldn't keep a job, but his mother over-compensated for this and smothered him with love. Direction people are usually raised in an insecure environment with a lot of love.

Competence

The fourth dominant trait is Competence, character-ized by a very strong desire to be excellent at what we do. A good student, one who frequently gets A's in high school, quickly becomes trapped in a competence cycle. She feels appreciated, loved, and respected when she's admired for how well she performs. This often leads her to specialize increasingly; because the more she specializes the more likely it is that people will admire her for her competency. Thirty years later she may end up as the world's top rocket expert, or heart surgeon.

George H. W. Bush, the father, would be a good example of a President whose dominant drive is com-petency. To be the best at what he does, whether it's as ambassador to the United Nations or head of the C.I.A., is his driving life force. Seldom will he venture off into flashy displays to impress people, or overt acts designed to gain popularity. In his mind, to be com-petent should be all that it takes to get him where he wants to go.

Bush was raised in a wealthy family with a lot of love. This is a typical environment for a child who will become a Competence person.

AC/DC is the key to understanding why you do what you do. It's why you are where you are, and how you're going to get where you want to go. Which are you? Is your driving life force the need for Accep-tance—the need for others to like you? Or striving for Control—the desire to have control over all elements of your life? Or Direction—the need to see your ideas and beliefs prevail? Or is it Competence—the need to be good at what you do?

You don't have to be a Freudian analyst to believe that what happens to you in your early life has a great deal of effect on your behavior as an adult. Jonathan Swift, the Irish author of *Gulliver's Travels*, said, "Give me a child for the first seven years, and you may do what you like with him afterwards," meaning that they're not going to change once they're older than seven. If you have children, you buy that, don't you? You can probably trace the characteristics that exist in your grown children all the way back to when they were no more than seven.

So let's look at these four dominant behavior traits and see how they emanate from things that happened when you were young.

To explore this with you, I must ask you two very personal and sensitive questions. Answer them openly and honestly. Since we're alone, forget what other people might think of your answer, especially your parents. OK? Let me give you the two questions first, and then I'll expand on them before you answer.

Question number one: Until you were seven, how *loved* did you feel?

Question number two: Until you were seven, how *secure* did you feel?

Question number one: Until you were seven, how loved did you feel? Of course, your first thought is to your parents and how much they loved you, and that's a very sensitive topic, isn't it? Not many people are going to say, "My Mommy didn't love me." However, there's much more to it than that. Apart from your relationship with your mother and father, consider your relationship with your brothers and sisters. Also, what was going on in the world at the time? For example, I was born in a London suburb just as the Battle of Britain was getting started. During the blitz of London, when bombs were falling every night, and the streets around us were collapsing, it was hard for me to feel loved, in spite of how wonderful my mother was to me. Be sure to consider all the circumstances of your childhood before you answer.

Be objective, and rate yourself on a scale of one to ten; with ten meaning, "Nobody could have been raised in a more loving environment," and one meaning, "Love? You mean children can feel loved?"

In the same way, think carefully about the second question: "Until you were seven, how secure did you feel?" Your parents don't have to raise you during a world war for you to feel insecure. Did your parents fight when you were young? Did you move a lot? How financially secure was your upbringing? When you've thought about it carefully, give yourself a score on a scale of one to ten. Ten meaning, "I don't remember being threatened by anything," and one meaning, "I never knew from one moment to the next what was going to happen."

You now have two scores, such as 4-3, or 4-7. Now let's interpret those scores. It'll be a lot easier for you to write these scores down. First, remember that the midpoint on a 1-10 scale is five and a half, not five. So five is low and six is high. Translate your score into words. A 4-3 score would be low-low. A 4-7 score would be low-high. An 8-2 score would be high low. A 7-6 score would be high-high. So you have four possibilities: low-low, low-high, high-low, and high-high. Do you know which you are? Are you still with me? If not go back over this section and try again. If you know which you are, I can now match you to your driving life force in my AC/DC formula. Low-low means that you're an Acceptance person. Low-high means that you're a Control person. High-low means that Direction is your driving life force. High-high means that you're a Competence person. The more extreme your numbers, the more pronounced will be the driving force. So an extreme low-high person would be someone with a 1-10 score, a real control freak. Someone with a 5-6 score would still be a control person, but less pronounced in their characteristics.

Someone with a dominant trait of either Acceptance or Direction, is probably a person who had an insecure childhood. They moved frequently when they were young, or were raised in an environment of poverty. This causes them to spend their lives seeking acceptance, either of themselves or their ideas.

On the other hand, people with a dominant trait of either Control or Competence, probably were raised in a very secure environment. They become high achievers, either as dominant leaders or highly competent people, because of this.

A person with the dominant traits of either Acceptance and Control would indicate a child raised with a low degree of love. A child who does not feel loved, will grow up still seeking love, or acceptance. Don't feel that this is all the parent's fault. They may have grown up feeling unloved because they were fat, ugly, or short; or a racial, religious or ethnic minority. This lack of love leads to a lack of self-confidence and the driving need to be accepted, or it could develop into the control trait. They want to control their environment because they don't have enough self-confidence in their ability to handle the unexpected.

Someone whose dominant traits are either Direction or Competence, probably had parents who raised him with a great deal of love. The high degree of self-esteem that a loving environment has given him develops the confidence to believe strongly in his ideas—a Direction person. Or it gives him the self-belief to be a high achiever, a Competence person.

To help you understand this, let me give you a profile of someone who represents each one of these driving life forces. These are the stories of Charlie, Elizabeth, David, and Karen. Four people from entirely different backgrounds whose upbringing deeply affected their future.

Charlie represents a child raised in an insecure environment with little love, who will become an Acceptance person. That would be you if your score was low-low. Lacking self-esteem and self-confidence, Charlie spends his life seeking the approval of others.

He was born in Philadelphia, the third child of an entrepreneurial real estate investor. The finances of his parents were on a perpetual roller coaster as they rode the cycles of the real estate market. Charlie seldom saw his father except when his mother was so angry with him that she asked his father to spank him. His mother was very highly strung and drank a lot to ease the tension. He grew up with the perception that his father was an angry person who was best avoided, and that things so easily upset his mother, that he needed to comfort her.

When he was five, the family's fortunes were low, so they lived in a cramped walk-up rental apartment in the South part of town. By the time he was nine, the family was wealthy and lived in a large home, and Charlie was attending a private school. Suddenly the real estate market turned, and his father had to file bankruptcy. The pressure caused his parents to divorce.

His mother took him out of private school and moved Charlie and his sisters to St. Louis, where his mother's family lived. She got a job on an aircraft manufacturing assembly line and after six months of living with his grandparents, they moved into a cramped rental house in the suburbs.

Charlie is now 35, and when he thinks of his childhood, he sees it as a very insecure, troubling time. While he thinks well of his parents, he never felt that they loved him very much. He doesn't think that they loved any of the children very much, but if they did, it was his two older sisters, not him.

He now works as an office manager for the same aircraft builder as his mother. As a manager, he is very much a consensus builder and gets everyone involved in decisions that affect the office. Three years ago the company fired him because he couldn't bring himself to lay off people during a cutback caused by the loss of a government contract to a competitor. But he pleaded his case with the Personnel director and they eventually reinstated him. His employees like him and the family atmosphere that he has created in the office. However, they criticize him behind his back because some employees take advantage of his good nature, and because he's reluctant to discipline poor workers.

He hates the thought that anybody in the world harbors bad feelings toward him, and plays golf once a week with a former employee whom he had to fire for stealing from the company.

His wife divorced him and he wonders if he'll ever fall in love again. She was eight years older and had two small children from a previous marriage. She became frustrated at his lack of assertiveness in climbing the corporate ladder, and left him for an older man, a building contractor from Kansas City. He feels terrible that she doesn't want him visiting her children, whom he loves deeply.

Charlie's life is a profile of an Acceptance person. Because he lacked both love and security as a child, he grew up desperately seeking the approval of others. You can see this in his preference for working at a large corporation, his scramble to get back on board when the company fired him, and the family atmosphere that exists in his department. If we were to look further into his marriage, we'd probably find that he didn't marry for the passion and excitement of a wild love affair, but because he saw himself moving into a non-threatening, comfortable environment by marrying an older woman who already had children.

Now let's look at Elizabeth, a child raised with little love in a secure environment who is destined to become a Control person. That would be you if your score was low-high. Over-compensating for her lack of self-esteem, Elizabeth wants to dominate others, and has to have her hand in everything. That's because she lacks the trust that a loving childhood would have given her.

Elizabeth was raised by a nanny on Fifth Avenue in New York, and spent weekends at her father's estate in Westchester. Her father is a famous theatrical producer, who spent little time with her when she was young, although he gave her every financial advantage.

She hasn't seen her mother since she was five years old, although her parents never divorced. Her father will never tell her what caused the split, although she has heard rumors that her mother lives outside Buenos Aires with an international playboy who raises polo ponies. She has also heard that her father has used his wealth and influence to stop her from getting a divorce. When she was a teenager she determined to track her mother down and uncover this mysterious family secret, but as time went by it took second place to her ambition as a career woman.

Her father is well known for his affairs with rich and famous women. Elizabeth doesn't mind that, and has spent many weekends in Bermuda or the Caribbean with her father and a famous actress or TV anchor-woman. Only when the girlfriend starts acting like a mother toward her does she rebel, and it has led to some violent scenes.

She was one of the first women to graduate from a former all-men's Ivy League College, and was vale-dictorian at the business school graduation. Her father's name helped her get a starting position with a Wall Street investment firm where she has become their top bond dealer. Her father was also very influential in referring clients to her. Elizabeth makes over a million dollars a year, but nobody likes her. Her five assistants regard her as a holy terror, and visibly shake with fear when she's having a bad day. She demands that all of her clients give her complete control over their accounts and will drop them if they question her decisions. The company partners once considered her for a partnership in the investment firm, which would have made her the most powerful woman on Wall Street. However, they quietly rejected her because they didn't see her as a team player.

She never married, nor has she had a long-term relationship with a man, although she has had many tempestuous affairs. She either clashes with men who have strong personalities, or has contempt for the ones who will let her control them.

Elizabeth is the product of a secure upbringing with little love. She has a high self-esteem because of her financially secure upbringing, but the lack of love in her life has given her a lack of trust in other people. Her Control tendency reveals itself in her relationships with both men and employees. Although she resents her father for the loss of her mother, she's pragmatic enough to live with it for the sake of his financial support and his influence over her career. She has become a classic Control person.

Now let's look at David, who was raised in an insecure environment with much love. David became a Direction person, who desperately wants to make his mark on life, and has the self-confidence to do it. That would be you if your score was high-low.

David is the son of a U.S. congressman from the San Francisco bay area. His father was a brilliant navy flier during the Korean War, and the first time David remembers meeting him was when the North Koreans released his father from a prisoner of war camp when David was eight. His father holds the distinction of being the only congressman ever voted out of office three times, and voted back in again in a subsequent election. Between elections his passion for politics would send him back out on the streets to press the flesh with the voters. Whenever he was back in office, however, he would always lose the financial support of some important backers because of his controversial stand on sensitive issues such as abortion and slashing defense costs.

The glue that held David's early life together was his mother, whom he idolizes. She has been the aide to a county supervisor for as long as David can remember, and is deeply involved in the local community. In the three two-year periods when his father was in congress, the family didn't move to Washington, although during school vacations he lived with his father in the capital.

When David thinks of his youth, it seems like a helter-skelter time of comings and goings. He has a very strong love for his mother, and a deep respect for his father's strength of character.

He married a young woman who heads up the consumer affairs division for the State of California, and who opened many political doors for him. They live in Sacramento.

He's a Democratic State senator and says in speeches that, "the excesses of the Reagan years," horrified him. He's a real crusader for free choice and healthcare reform. He's been gathering support for a run in the Governor's race next year, and dreams about it being only a stepping-stone to the White House. Deeply concerned about the direction of the country, he sees no one else in politics that has his commitment to serving the public rather than the needs of special interest groups. He feels fortunate to have a wife who shares his concerns; because in his heart he knows that his drive for social reform would take precedence over his marriage.

David is clearly a Direction person. The love of his parents, especially his mother, has given him a great amount of self-confidence. But the chaotic insecurity of his childhood means that he lacks a deep inner self-esteem. He has a strong desire to prove himself and make his mark on the world. You can see his Direction tendencies in his politically expedient choice of a wife, and concern about political issues that are beyond the scope of a state senator.

Finally Karen, who was raised in a secure environment with much love, and is now a Competence person. That would be you if you have a high-high score. Karen doesn't need to prove herself in a flamboyant way because she has high self-esteem, so she quietly goes about the job of showing herself how much she can excel.

Karen spent her entire childhood in a large home on the outskirts of Milwaukee. Her father is a top executive with a life insurance company, who married her mother after they met in business school at Stanford University. Although her mother was a brilliant student, she never pursued a business career, because she saw more value in raising a family. Karen is the fourth of six children, all of whom get along well. She thinks of her childhood as a whirl of exciting things such as violin and ballet classes, and vacations in Colorado with the whole family riding horses together.

When she was ten, she went with her father for his three-day executive check up at the Mayo Clinic, and spent many hours with the nurses there, who fell in love with her. From that moment on everyone in the family knew that Karen would one day go into medicine. It was a proud moment for her parents when Karen graduated near the top of her class from Stanford Medical School.

They thought she would return to Milwaukee and go into practice there, but a research facility in San Diego tempted her with a grant for graduate studies. Three years later she quietly went to work for them and was responsible for isolating the AIDS virus, although she let the head of the facility take credit saying he would be able to generate more funding from the publicity.

Happily married to the owner of a marina in La Jolla, she has two children.

Karen is a Competence person. Her loving and secure upbringing lead her to want nothing more in life than to explore what she sees as her God given talent. You can see that in the way she made her own career decisions, both to go into medicine and pursue a future in research. She passed up the chance for fame and fortune with her research breakthrough, in favor of doing what would be best for the project. Although she probably could have attracted a wealthy powerful husband, she chose instead someone who loved what he did. She seeks neither wealth nor fame, and all her contentment comes from knowing that she's a good wife, mother, and researcher.

What characteristics did you see in yourself as I told you about Charlie, Elizabeth, David, and Karen? Are you like office manager Charlie and think the most important thing is that other people accept you? Or maybe stock broker Elizabeth, who has driving ambition but difficulty getting close to people? Perhaps you're more like congressional representative David, with a drive to make your views heard by the rest of the world. Or perhaps you identified most with medical researcher Karen, whose greatest pride is in doing things right.

Where do you see yourself? Knowing whether you're an Acceptance, Control, Direction or Competence person is the key to understanding your behavior.

Realize that each of these four characteristics has a positive and a negative side. As you listened to the four people's stories, I'm sure that you saw more positives in the one who is most like you, didn't you? However, if you look at them objectively, you'll see that all four have positives and negatives.

The Acceptance person's positive is that they're likable people. They always build consensus around ideas, and very seldom ruffle any body's feathers. You can count on them to resolve conflict smoothly and be a good peacemaker. They get things done because they're good with people.

The negative side of an Acceptance person is that they're reluctant to take a stand and fight for what they want. They're not the kind of person you would want to lead an army into battle or lead a company out of bankruptcy. Their desire to be liked causes them to avoid conflict.

The Control person is brilliant at getting things done, as long as they have complete charge of the project. This is a Ross Perot, working miracles as long as he has autonomy, but getting so frustrated with politics—where he would have to do more persuading than commanding—that he got out of the Presidential race quickly. A revealing look at his personality came when he and GM chairperson Roger Smith were to attend a dinner with the management of their new Saturn subsidiary. Perot told Roger Smith that he had bought 500 copies of *Leadership Secrets of Attila the Hun* to distribute at the dinner. Smith was beside himself and sent his public relations man to talk Perot out of the idea.

Control people are terrible at delegating, and quickly alienate other people, although those people may admire them very much.

The Direction person shines when they're swimming against the tide. This is Winston Churchill in the 1930s desperately trying to warn England of the Nazi menace or Ralph Nader on a one-man crusade for safer automobiles.

Where they fail to shine is in the details. In World War One, Winston Churchill was the father of a new secret weapon that would create the turning point in the war against Germany. To keep secret what he was doing, he code-named the project Tank, and he let out the rumor that they were making water carriers for the Czar of Russia. The name tank eventually stuck for the armored vehicle he was developing. On August 8, 1918, 456 of them broke through the German lines north of Paris. They advanced six miles in minutes, which was an incredible victory for those times. The problem was that he hadn't thought what to do next, as the tanks roared past the German front lines with no infantry or cavalry able to support their advance. However, the tank was to the First World War what the atom bomb was to the second. Once the Germans saw what it could do, they realized that they could never win the war.

The positive side of the Competence person is that they're thorough, professional in everything they do, and can always be counted on to turn in a superb performance. They're outstanding in occupations that allow little room for error, like medicine, the law, and design engineering.

The negative is that they're not great leaders or innovators. They thrive well in an arena that requires perfection and reliability, but don't expect the dramatic flair that inspires other people to rise up and follow them.

We all have strengths in our behavior, and we have weaknesses. In this chapter, I've laid the groundwork for you to understand how you got where you are today. Only when you fully understand why you do what you do, will you fully understand how you're going to get where you want to go. Achieving your full potential is less a matter of eliminating weaknesses, than it is in fine-tuning your ambitions so that they flow with your strengths.

In our next chapter, I'll teach you how always to behave with the highest level of enthusiastic optimism, even in the face of discouragement. You know how important it is to have an enthusiastic approach to life don't you? Well, I'll show you how to do it, in chapter three.

Chapter Three

How to Stay Enthusiastic

In this chapter, I'm going to show you how to maintain enthusiastic behavior every hour of your life, regardless of the setbacks life may hand you. In short, what I have to tell you is this: when something good happens you should P! P! P! and when something bad happens you should I! I! I! I'm sure that doesn't make any sense to you now, but in half an hour it will, and I promise it will change your life.

Since this is an advanced course in personal achievement, I assume you know the basics. You know to have a written goal that you always carry with you in your pocket or purse. The goal must have a time deadline. You must know the steps that lead to your goal, so that you're not just sitting around waiting for a miracle to happen. You know the importance of constantly visualizing yourself as having achieved that goal. You know to keep your attitude up by treating every adversity as a learning experience in disguise.

However, if you're doing all that and still get depressed at times, then what? The problem is that life hands you some big dollops of discouragement from time to time and you need more than motivation to keep you going.

Listen to the story of Mrs. Linda Eagleson, who lives in Lynwood, California. I've changed her name to protect her privacy, but the story is true. Lynwood is next to south-central Los Angeles and the home of several youth gangs that plague the area. Drive-by killings now take the lives of over 700 people a year in the county, so the press seldom bothers to report them. One day a volley of gunshots from a passing car killed Mrs. Eagleson's 21-year-old son Joe, an auto-body repair worker. Although Joe wasn't a member of a gang, a friend of his saw the killing and confirmed that Joe knew who killed him. However, the friend was afraid of gang reprisals and refused to testify, so the police didn't do anything about the killing. This was a devastating way to lose a son.

However Linda Eagleson believed in positive thinking, and knew the answer to her grief was to turn this negative experience into something positive. She went to her local access television station and talked them into putting a show on the air called *Drive-by Agony.*

Every week she would host her television show, which featured interviews with parents of other youths killed in drive-by shootings. With over two drive-by shootings a day in her neighborhood, she never had to search for guests. She always had a list of grief-stricken parents who wanted to appear. The program did a great job of raising public awareness of a problem so commonplace, that the rest of the media seldom bothered to report it.

Three years later, her program was appearing twice a week, and Linda was busy planning an anti-crime rally to take place outside the Criminal Courts building in Los Angeles. While her TV program was on the air, she got devastating news. Her only other son Greg, who was studying to become a probation officer, was in the emergency ward. Gang members had shot him four times in the back as he was trying to run away from them. By the time she could get to the hospital, he was dead.

"My God," she screamed, "is there something else I'm supposed to be doing? Or am I only supposed to be a martyr?" However, she pressed on with her television show and the anti-crime rally, saying, "I'll be damned if my son will become just another body."

The point is: how do we keep a positive attitude under the onslaught of such terrible tragedy? You'll probably never have two children murdered, but I've never met a person who hasn't had to face some kind of devastating tragedy in their lives. If you're to become all that you're capable of becoming, you must learn to control your behavior even when the worst happens. To Linda Eagleson, it was the senseless killing of her sons.

To you it may be no more than your boss passing you over for a promotion, your lover walking out on you, or losing your home or job. These things can happen to us all and we must learn to let these problems slide off us.

In this chapter, I'm going to teach you specific steps that will train you how to react to the events in your life, so that you're always able to behave enthusiastically.

Later, when I teach you behavior shaping, I'll show you how our reactions to events can lead to learned despair. For now, just accept this: one of the greatest lessons of life is that it really doesn't matter what happens to you, what matters is how you react to what happens to you. A hopeless alcoholic can have identical twins. One may grow up to be an alcoholic also, saying, "What did you expect, my father always drank, so of course I'm going to grow up with bad habits too." The other twin may become a lifelong teetotaler saying, "Well of course I wouldn't drink, I saw what it did to my father." In almost any seriously dysfunctional family, you'll find that one child will react by becoming very responsible and controlling, and the other child will become irresponsible. They're reacting in opposite ways to the same event.

You have only to look at the early lives of recent Presidents to believe this. Richard Nixon's father was a bitter, violent man who failed at everything he tried, and worked out his frustrations by beating his sons. Gerald Ford's stepfather adopted him when he was three, but he didn't know that his mother had been lying to him until his real father walked up to him on the street when he was sixteen. Jimmy Carter's father was a strong domineering bigot who frequently beat his son with a peach switch. Ronald Reagan's father was a hopeless alcoholic who drifted from town to town. This shows that a terrible upbringing doesn't have to stop you from achieving.

It's not what happens to you, it's how you react to what happens to you and consequently how you behave in response to what happens. To be more precise, the essential thing is how you interpret what happens to you, because your behavior depends on your interpretation of what happens, not on what actually happened.

Let me give you a simple example of that. I own a second home at beautiful Lake Arrowhead in the mountains outside Los Angeles, that I let friends and business acquaintances use. It occasionally snows up there during the winter, so they may get snowed-in and have to extend their stay for a day or two. The differences in reaction that people have to this event is astonishing. Some are angry, and never want to go there again, even in the summer. Others think that being snowed-in is a great adventure, and always want to go up there during the winter.

These scenarios have three stages.

- The event, which was getting snowed-in.
- How they interpreted the event, as either a nuisance or an adventure.
- Their behavior after the event—to return to the cabin or not.

On the surface, Karl Menninger was accurate when he said that what happens to you doesn't matter, that it's how you react to what happens that counts. However, it's an oversimplification, because he skipped the middle step. It's how you interpret the event that counts. That may seem like splitting hairs to you, but it's an essential step in our journey to success.

Now I'm going to teach you how to change the way you interpret what happens to you, because it's a key to controlling your behavior. I based this on the breakthrough research of Dr. Martin Seligman, at the University of Pennsylvania. He wrote a great book about it called *Learned Optimism*. I think you'll want to read it, and I'll tell you more about it later. Your behavior following what happens to you is dependent upon the three "P"s and the three "I"s. Let me go through it briefly and then I'll go back over it in detail.

The first "P" stands for Permanence, and the first "I" stands for the opposite, Impermanence. Permanence refers to whether you consider an event is a permanent condition or only a temporary occurrence. Therefore, it refers to time. The optimist sees good things as always happening again in similar circumstances, and sees bad things as a one-time fluke. The pessimist sees good things as a one-time fluke and bad things as always recurring. The optimists saw getting snowed-in at the cabin as a one-time event; the pessimists saw it as something that was likely to happen every time they went there.

The second "P" stands for Personal, and the second "I" stands for Impersonal. The optimist sees good events as being to their credit and bad things as being someone else's fault. The pessimist sees good things as someone else's doing and bad things as their fault. So the snowed-in optimist thinks, "Roger should have told me to bring chains." The snowed-in pessimist thinks, "This is all my fault, I was stupid to come up here."

The third "P" stands for Pervasive, and the third "I" stands for Isolated. The optimist sees good things as an indication of good things happening all over, and sees bad things as an isolated event. The pessimist sees good things as an isolated event and bad things as an indication that bad things are happening everywhere. The snowed-in optimist thinks, "The next time we come to Lake Arrowhead in winter, we'll rent a cabin on the main road, and this won't happen." The snowed-in pessimist thinks, "Everybody's having the same problem, so I'll never come here in winter again."

What I've given you was such a quick run through of what Dr. Seligman's research revealed, and I can understand if I confused you. So, let me go through it again in more detail. Let's take a good event and follow it through each of the three stages: the event, the interpretation of the event, and the behavior following the interpretation.

For example: Stage One: the good event. A salesperson works hard all week, and on Friday lands a big sale. Stage Two: the interpretation of what happened. The optimist sees permanence; "I know how to sell this now, so I won't have any more trouble." The pessimist sees impermanence; "Well finally I got lucky." Stage

Three: the behavior following the interpretation. The optimist can't wait until Monday morning when he'll be able to make another sale. The pessimist drags himself to work, doubting he'll be lucky enough to make another sale.

Remember that a pessimist is someone who feels bad when he feels good—for fear he'll feel better when things get worse. An optimist is someone who feels good when he feels bad—in the hope that he'll feel better when things get worse.

Here's an example of reactions to a bad event: Stage One, the bad event: a man tries to record a program on his cable TV box but when he sits down to watch it, all he gets is snow. Stage Two, the interpretation of what happened: the pessimist sees it as permanent and thinks, "I'll never get the hang of this downloading." The optimist sees it as temporary and thinks, "I must not have set it right this time." Stage Three, the behavior following the interpretation: the pessimist quits trying to record programs, and the optimist figures out the mistake he made and keeps on trying.

So, the first thing you must do is train yourself to interpret all good events as permanent. Remember that permanence has to do with time, not space. A good example of this would be to say to yourself: "This person was interested in what I had to say, therefore I will always have interesting things to say." If you had a slightly different reaction, you'd be missing the point. If, instead of saying, "This person was interested in what I had to say, therefore I will always have interesting things to say," you said, "therefore everyone will be interested in what I have to say." That would be an optimistic reaction but you're not referring to permanence. Permanence has to do with time, not space.

Let me illustrate that point again. Listen to this example and see if you can add an interpretation that would indicate permanence. Here's the event: you say to yourself, "This person wanted to go out on a date with me." What should your interpretation be?

If you said, "Therefore this person will always say *yes* when I ask them for a date," you had the right response. If you said, "Therefore everyone will say *yes* when I ask them," that's great, but you're referring to pervasiveness not permanence.

Let me give you one more example of permanence versus impermanence. Let's say that you have a secretary who always seems to have a backlog of work. When you need something done right away, it's hard for you to talk her into stopping what she's doing to take care of it. But this time you try a little different approach and she says, "No problem, I'll take care of it right now." That's the event, and to interpret this good event as a permanent condition you should think, "That's great! From now on, I'll always be able to get her to do that." Not, "This will work on anyone." That is an optimistic reaction, and there's nothing wrong with it, but it's important for you to understand that permanence refers to time and pervasiveness refers to space.

So the first thing we've learned about interpretation of an event is that an optimist sees any good event as permanent, that it will always recur, and the pessimist sees good events as impermanent or unlikely to recur. Now let's turn that around and look at bad events. When bad things happen the opposite is true. When a bad event happens, the optimist sees it as impermanent, unlikely to recur. The pessimist sees it as permanent, likely to recur.

Let's follow a bad event through the three stages. First, the bad event: a salesperson is cold calling on the telephone, and the customer hangs up on him. Second, the interpretation of what happened: the optimist sees it as impermanent, for example, "That was unfortunate, I reached that person at the wrong time." The pessimist sees it as permanent, for example, "That person will never buy from me." Third, the behavior following the interpretation: the optimist tries the call again later. The pessimist crosses that person off his list.

Here's another example. First, the bad event: a boss asks an employee to work on Sunday, to help push through a delayed project. The employee says, no, explaining that she has to teach a Sunday school class at her church. Second, the interpretation: the optimist sees that as meaning that only that one Sunday was a problem. The pessimist sees the employee as never being willing to work on a Sunday. Third, the behavior following the interpretation: the optimist maintains good relations with the employee, and doesn't hesitate to ask her to work on Sunday the next time it's important. The pessimist assumes that the employee is never willing to work on Sunday, becomes afraid that he'll be accused of religious discrimination if he does, and develops bad feelings about her.

So far, I've covered only the first of the three "P"s, and the first of the three "I"s. To be an optimist you should always interpret good events as permanent, and bad events as impermanent. Avoid pessimistic interpretation of events, which is to see good events as impermanent ("I got lucky that time.") and bad events as permanent ("I'll never get the hang of this.")

Now let's move to the second of the three "P"s, which stands for Personal. The opposite of that is the second "I," which stands for Impersonal. When good things happen to an optimist, he or she sees them as personal, that they were responsible for it happening. When good things happen to a pessimist, he or she sees the other person as being responsible.

Let's follow that concept through the three stages. First, the good event: a salesperson in a sporting goods store talks to a customer who came in to buy a fishing lure. He ends up selling him a new rod and reel, and a boat, motor and trailer. Second, the interpretation of the event: the optimist says, "Wow, am I a great salesperson." The pessimist says, "Wow, was that guy a soft touch!" Third, the behavior following the interpretation: the optimist keeps trying to sell a boat to every customer. The pessimist thinks it was a fluke, and doesn't try that hard any more.

Here are more examples. The optimist goes to sell his house, and finds that it has gone way up in value. He says, "I really bought the right house, didn't I?" The pessimist in the same situation responds impersonally by saying, "Real estate values have really gone up in this town."

A business executive hears that her company has had a banner year. If she's an optimist she says, "I really contributed to this great year." If she's a pessimist she says, "I'm lucky to be with a company that is doing so well."

To recap, the second of the three "P"s, which stands for Personal, says that an optimist sees good things as personal, that they caused the good event. However the pessimist sees the good event and interprets it in an impersonal way, such as, "I was lucky to be in the right place when this happened."

Their reaction to a bad event is just the opposite. The optimist sees the bad event as impersonal, not caused by them. The pessimist sees the bad event as personal, their fault.

Let's follow a bad event through the three stages. First, the bad event: a vice-president of a company hopes to become president when his boss retires. However it doesn't happen and the board of directors goes to the outside instead. Second, the interpretation of the event: the optimist says, "The board of directors made a big mistake." The pessimist says, "What a fool I was to think they'd pick me." Third, the behavior following the interpretation: the optimist keeps on positioning himself to be next in line for the job, or starts maneuvering to become president of another company. The pessimist sees himself as never being presidential material and gives up trying.

Let's discuss this last point for a moment. If you're familiar with my other books and programs, you know that I'm a big believer in taking responsibility for what happens to you. That's because every time I've counseled someone who's not achieving his full potential, I always find that he's blaming other people for what's gone wrong with his life. If he was fired from a job, it's because the boss was an idiot, not because he didn't work hard enough. If he flunks a test, it was because the professor was unrealistic, not because he didn't study hard enough. If a marriage fails, it was his wife's fault, not his. I once counseled a young man who had worked at 35 different jobs in the 8 years since he'd left high school. I had him list each of the jobs and the reason he left. In 32 cases, he left because the boss was an idiot! Isn't that a remarkable coincidence? There are probably only about 40 complete idiots running businesses in the country, and he'd already worked for 32 of them! I told him that the price he must pay for the things he wanted out of life was that he must accept responsibility for what happens and quit blaming other people. I am a big believer in accepting personal responsibility for what happens to you. So, why am I now saying that to be an optimist, you should only take responsibility for the good things, and never the bad? How can I put those two together?

The answer is that it depends on whether the person is in a rational state of mind or not. A pessimistic person will take on far too much responsibility for what happens to them. One of their parents dies and they become obsessed with the thought that if they had cared more, it wouldn't have happened. A woman's husband drinks too much, and she thinks it's because she's failed him, and she becomes codependent. A child gets bad grades, and the parents see themselves to blame.

If your thinking is perfectly rational, and you're normally very upbeat and enthusiastic, it's OK to take responsibility when things go wrong. Since you have just learned to interpret bad things as temporary, it's not going to last anyway. However, if what I'm telling you in this chapter interests you because you'd like to be more optimistic in your thinking, try taking **less** responsibility for the events in your life.

Something that has puzzled psychologists for a long time is that women are far more likely to get depressed than men are. In this country about 5 percent of men are clinically depressed, but 10 percent of women suffer from the disease. Research is now indicating that we learn to blame others or blame ourselves from either our parents or our teachers. It appears that in the past, both parents and teachers treated boys differently from girls when it came to blaming them when they misbehaved at home or performed poorly in school. With boys, parents and teachers tend to focus on the behavior, and tell the boy, "You did poorly, and you can do better." Girls are much more likely to get blamed when they behave badly or poorly, and they tell told, "You did poorly and you'll never do anything right." Experts call this dispositional attribution, which means blaming the person rather than the circumstances. We all tend to blame the person more than the circumstances. We see someone speeding and automatically think that they're behaving irresponsibly, rather than considering the reason they may be driving fast. If we watch a television quiz show, we tend to over-emphasize the ability of the contestant to answer the question, and under-emphasize the difficulty of the question. It appears however, that dispositional attribution is much higher toward girls than it is toward boys. It appears that culturally, we care more about what boys do, but are more concerned about what girls become. Hopefully this prejudice is on its way out, but emotional development experts such as Carol Dweck believe that this is the reason women suffer depression twice as much as men. If you don't believe me, try this out on your own children. Ask you son why he didn't do something well and he's likely to tell you, "Because I was busy and didn't concentrate." Ask your daughter and she's more likely to say, "I've never been good at that kind of thing." By the way, I realize that this is controversial, but I like to hear from you, so I always want to give you a reason to email me!

Let's recap. So far, I've covered the first two "P"s and the first two "I"s of optimistic thinking. Optimistic people see good events as permanent and personal. They see bad events as impermanent and impersonal. Pessimistic people have this backward: they see good events as impermanent and impersonal, and they see bad events as permanent and personal.

Now let's look at the third set of "P"s and "I"s. The third "P" stands for pervasive, which means it affects everything. The third "I" stands for isolated, meaning just applying to this particular event.

When a good event happens to an optimist, he or she sees it as meaning that things are good all over. When a good event happens to a pessimist, he or she sees it as an isolated event. Pervasiveness relates to space, not time. "It's happening all over," rather than, "this happened, so it's likely to happen again."

Let's follow that concept through the three stages. First, the good event: a sales manager at a tractor company gets a big order from a construction company. Second, the interpretation of the event: the optimist says, "That's terrific, the construction business must be really picking up." The pessimist says, "The construction company must have just landed a big contract." Third, the behavior following the interpretation: the optimist rallies the sales force, tells them the recession is over and that they should catch the wave of prosperity. The pessimist is glad to have the business, but doesn't do anything because he doesn't see any upward trend taking place.

Here is another example. The optimist gets a good job offer and sees it as pervasive: "the job market must be great right now." The pessimist sees it as isolated: "I was lucky to be offered such a great opportunity."

Now let's turn that around and see that the behavior following a bad event is just the opposite. The optimist sees the bad event as isolated: "Just because this bad thing happened, it doesn't mean it's bad all over." The pessimist sees the bad event as pervasive, an indication that things are terrible all over.

Let's follow a bad event through the three stages. First, the bad event: an aircraft manufacturer loses a big order to a European consortium. Second, the interpretation of the event: the optimist says, "We lost that one, and we'll work harder to be sure it doesn't happen again." The pessimist says, "Looks like the days when American companies can dominate the aircraft business are over." Third, the behavior following the interpretation: the optimist intensifies training for his sales force to be sure they don't let another sale go to the competition. The pessimist sees the writing on the wall and pushes the company to start downsizing.

Let's recap again what Dr. Seligman's research revealed. Optimistic people see good events as permanent, personal and pervasive. They see bad events as impermanent, impersonal, and isolated. Pessimistic people have this backward: they see good events as impermanent, impersonal, and isolated, and they see bad events as permanent, personal and pervasive.

What I've given you here is a blueprint for optimistic behavior regardless of what happens to you, and that's essential if you're to achieve your full potential. It's also a blueprint for changing your behavior. You must be willing to change the way you do things. To change your behavior you must be willing to do two things. First, you must be proactive, not reactive, to the things that happen to you. That means understanding that the event is not the issue, it's how you interpret the event that counts. Second, you must train yourself never to see things as pervasive or permanent.

The other reason what we've covered here is important to your future is that it makes you a much better manager. If you can train your people to see good things as Permanent, Personal and Pervasive, and bad things as Impermanent, Impersonal and Isolated, you will be able to dramatically improve their performance. Let me give you a simple example. You run a store and hire a new clerk. It's probable that during their first week on the job they're going to make some mistakes, right? With one sentence, you can change their reaction to these mistakes. Say to them during training, "Don't worry if you make mistakes during your first week—everybody does it." In one sentence you've told them that the mistakes are Impermanent because they only happen when they're new, that they're Impersonal because it happens to everybody, and that they're Isolated to the first week. Incidentally, you'll find that generally speaking this has a bigger impact on the male employees than it does on females. Not because men understand it better, but because when men get into trouble they tend to withdraw. When women have trouble, they tend to share. So Charlie is back in the lunchroom with his head in his hands thinking, "I'll never get the hang of this job. They're probably going to fire me any minute." Charlene, on the other hand, is back in the lunchroom saying, "I feel awful that I'm having trouble with this." Charlene's new friends remind her of what you taught her in training, "Don't worry, it's only because you're new, everybody goofs up when they first start. By next week you'll have the hang of it."

She's getting reinforcement that problems are Impermanent, Impersonal, and Isolated.

What I've covered in this chapter also gives you the formula for hope. People who are full of hope see good things as permanent and pervasive: "The economy's booming and it's never going to slow down." And they see bad things are impermanent and isolated: "Sure we're in a recession, but it never lasts forever, and not everybody is being hurt by it."

All this may not be easy to grasp when you first hear it, but it's the foundation for changing your behavior. I need you to be comfortable with it before we move on. A good test of comprehension is: would you feel comfortable explaining what you learned in this chapter to someone else? If not, I urge you to review this chapter again before you go on to chapter four.

If you'd like to learn more about training yourself to interpret properly the events in your life, I highly recommend Dr. Martin Seligman's great book, *Learned Optimism,* published by Alfred A. Knopf. His writing style is very entertaining, and I know you'll really enjoy reading the book.

If you're comfortable that when something good happens you should P! P! P! and when something bad happens you should I! I! I!, let's move on to chapter four. That's where I'll start teaching you how to shape your behavior.

Chapter Four

The Magic of Behavior Shaping

So far, I've only laid the foundation for learning how to shape your future by shaping your behavior.

First, I stressed that for things to change in your life, you must change your behavior. Positive thinking and other forms of metaphysical thought are helpful but alone they will not change your life. Cognitive analysis, to find out why you do what you do, is only useful if it leads to a change in behavior. Behavior shapers believe that if you structure your behavior so that it's effectively reinforced, a positive attitude will follow. For you to become all you're capable of becoming, your behavior must change. True, it's also essential that you are thinking change—that you become smarter—but that's only an intermediate step. Ultimately, for things to change in your life, you must change what you do; not only what you think.

Second, I taught you about the driving life force that controls your behavior. Knowing and understanding your driving life force is essential to understanding the reasons for your present behavior. If you understand what drives you—Acceptance, Control, Direction, or Competence—you can fine-tune your ambitions so that they flow with your strengths.

Third, I taught you how to maintain enthusiastic behavior, even in the face of discouragement. The key is how we interpret what happens to us. Interpret good things as Permanent, Personal, and Pervasive. Interpret bad things as Impermanent, Impersonal, and Isolated. When something good happens you should P! P! P! and when something bad happens you should I! I! I!

With those three basics out of the way, it's time to get into the heart of **MOVING BEYOND GOALS TO THE NEXT LEVEL OF ACCOMPLISHMENT,** which is learning the skill of behavior shaping. In the next few chapters, I'm going to teach you that your behavior—what you do—is never an isolated event. Your behavior doesn't happen in a vacuum. There is a chain of events that cause you to do the things you do. To alter your behavior, you must change that chain of events. You can use it on other people too because the same techniques will work to change the behavior of the people whose support you need.

The first thing to learn about behavior is this: *what you do is not who you are.* The world would love to tell you otherwise, but it's not true. The world would say that if you steal, you're a crook; that if you drink too much, you're a drunk, and that if you fail, you're a failure. I say that's not true, because I believe that people can change, and I believe in redemption. Only if you are unable to change your behavior of stealing, should you be labeled a crook; only if you are unable to control your drinking, should you be labeled a drunk; and only if you fail at *everything* you do, should you be called a failure. Just because you behave in a certain way in a certain circumstance doesn't mean you'll behave the same way again, even in similar circumstances. If you seemed to have reached a plateau in your accomplishments, I suggest you evaluate your talents and abilities and see if you haven't labeled yourself. Perhaps you tried selling encyclopedias door to door when you were in college and the people rejected you so much that you never tried selling again. Perhaps your company promoted you into a management position too early in your career. You didn't do well, so you've labeled yourself as a poor manager. Perhaps your marriage collapsed and you've labeled yourself as a poor marriage prospect.

In our society, we love labels. It isn't that way in other cultures. A few years ago I spent a week on the island of Borneo, and hired a guide to take me on a canoe up the Skrang River to stay at one of the native's mysterious longhouses. These community houses are unique to the remote areas of Borneo. They're called longhouses because they may start as a home for four or five families, but as the community grows, the house grows. When two of the children marry, they build an additional room on the end of the house. Over the decades, the house gets longer and longer. The one at which I stayed had over forty families living in it.

These people were headhunters until just before World War Two, when a cook stole a bottle of whisky from the District Commissioner. One of the natives ran across the cook in the forest, propped up against a tree drinking the whisky. Eager to right the wrong, he did what he thought would be proper. As the commissioner and his wife were sipping drinks with friends on their verandah, he walked into their garden with the whisky bottle in one hand and the cook's head in the other. He thought it would thrill them. The commissioner's wife fainted and her husband sent the man off to jail for two years. This was how the natives in the longhouse learned that head hunting was no longer acceptable. However, that didn't stop the old men of the long house from proudly showing me the heads that they had captured when they were young.

Primitive societies such as these seem to avoid labeling people the way that we do. Just because the elders of the village were headhunters during their youth, when headhunting was an accepted form of behavior, it doesn't make them murderers today.

Avoid the temptation to label yourself. If you label yourself based on your behavior today, you make it so much harder for you to change your behavior in the future. What you *do* is not the same thing as who you *are*. Knowing that what you do is different from who you are, keeps your thinking fresh and stops you from mentally congealing.

Labeling other people is unfair and discourteous. Labeling ourselves is incredibly self-destructive, for two reasons. If we give ourselves a limiting label, it closes the door on all we might become in the future. Here are some examples of limiting labels:

- I can't take the stress of a top management job, so I'll stay in middle management.
- I don't have a college education, so I can only go so far.
- With my looks, I'm not going to attract the most desirable partner.

Obviously, limiting labels like these lower your self-image and stop you from accomplishing anything beyond the new parameters that they set for you.

However, there's another type of labeling that can be even more self-destructive. That's to label yourself ambitiously high. For example, you give $5 to a homeless person and label yourself as a good person rather than someone who has just done something good. Here are some examples of this type of thinking:

- I am a generous person, rather than one who sometimes acts generously.
- I am a great parent, boss, salesperson, or secretary; rather than: I handle some of the tasks involved well.

- I am a perfectionist, rather than someone who tries to do their best.

What's so wrong with labeling yourself as a perfectionist? Isn't this what self-image psychology is all about? Raise your self-image and you expand your parameters, right? Yes, but it can also give you problems. What if you label yourself as a generous person, for example, and then later you're not able to be so generous? What if you've labeled yourself as a great person, and then you mess up? It can be devastating to you. Comparing yourself to the label you've given yourself and coming up short can lead to depression. This is another skirmish between cognitive psychology and behavioral psychology, isn't it? The cognitive therapist says, "Learn how to feel good about yourself." I say, "Learn to feel good about what you do." In my book, it's OK to say, "I want to be great at what I do." It's when you try to label who you are, by saying, "I'm going to be a perfect person," that you run into trouble.

In behavior shaping, we never consider just the behavior, because it leads to labeling. We always consider the behavior in relationship to what happened before, and what happens after. We call what happened before the behavior the antecedent, and what happens after the behavior, we call the consequence. The sequence is A-B-C: Antecedent, Behavior, Consequence. Later I'll teach you that, in spite of what you might think, behavior is a product of its consequence and not its antecedent. It sounds weird, but you do what you do because of what happens after, not because of what happens before.

Isn't it fascinating to watch people label themselves, when they should be evaluating only their behavior? I was fifteen when I first started noticing it. I spent a summer working at a carnival in Littlehampton, which is a beach resort not far from my home in the south of England. They put me to work at a game of chance where people would pay to feed balls into a fake duck's mouth. I supervised a long line of ducks that were all swiveling back and forth. When the ball came out of its rear end, the duck was still swiveling furiously back and forth, so they never knew into which slot it would fall. Hey, don't laugh! This is my great humble beginning story! The players paid for six balls, and they would feed them into the duck's mouth and wait for them to drop into slots marked with a score. Then I would add up the score and match it to the prizes lined up behind me. It took me days to figure out why nobody ever won a big prize. It was virtually impossible to get them to add up to the number that won a big prize. The only way you could do it was to get each one of the six balls into a designated slot. That's as close to impossible as you can get, when you're talking about a random roll of a ball through the insides of a duck. It wasn't hard to make it add up to one less or one more, but not the exact number. The players didn't figure it out because nobody ever planned their strategy before they started playing. They would always drop a few balls in, trying to get the higher numbers. Then they would add up how much they had so far, and compare it to the numbers on the prizes to see how much more they needed. When they realized that they couldn't win one of the big prizes, they would attempt to get one of the less valuable ones. When I realized the deception, I asked for a transfer and spent the rest of the summer outside running a train for toddlers.

The interesting thing was the reaction of the players when they failed at something that, unknown to them, was impossible. The smart ones would never let their failure make them feel bad. They would put it down to bad luck. However, people who habitually felt poorly about themselves, would always say, "I'm not good at this sort of thing." Or, what's worse, "I never win anything." For these people, it wasn't a matter of what they did in a specific environment at a specific time. It immediately became a matter of who they are and who they always have been and always will be. Even in something as inconsequential as guiding a ball out of the rear end of a duck, they would label themselves as a failure!

If a salesperson who thinks that way does poorly when he first makes a presentation to a big account, his immediate response is: "I'm no good at selling big accounts." Whereas a behavior shaper would automatically relate the result to the situation, and say: "I did a lousy job preparing for that presentation, so the result was poor. But why did I do such a poor job preparing? Because in the past, when I sold to small accounts, I've been rewarded even though I didn't prepare well.

Big account selling must be a different league. I'm not going to be rewarded unless I prepare better. Next time I'll do a better job of preparing, and I'll make the sale."

The first thing I want you to learn about behavior shaping is to quit labeling yourself. Instead, start relating your results to your behavior. Since you can always change your behavior, you can always change the results. With that in mind, now let's start looking at how you can change your behavior.

Let me tell you about a trip I took that really drove home the power of behavior shaping. One beautiful spring evening Pat and Monty Roberts invited me to come to their ranch to see for myself their now famous method of breaking horses. They own Flag-is-Up Farms near Solvang, California, one of the top horse breeding and training farms on the West Coast. It's located in the beautiful Santa Ynez Valley just north of Santa Barbara. Solvang is a popular tourist area because most of the people who live there are Danish and the entire village is designed with a Danish motif. It's full of picturesque windmills, bake shops and souvenir stores.

I had heard about the remarkable work that Monty Roberts does training horses, and the chance to see a firsthand demonstration excited me. Pat Roberts taught me more about behavior in 34 minutes than I had learned in a lifetime. What I learned that beautiful spring evening was an incredible lesson in how we can train ourselves and others to do things that appear to be impossible.

Because my brother trained racehorses in England, I knew a little about how trainers break horses so that jockeys can ride them. I'm sure you're familiar with the cruel way that cowboys broke horses in the old West. They dragged the unwilling horse to a paddock and with several ranch hands holding it down, pulled a bridle over its head and forced a bit into its mouth. Sometimes they put a mask over its head so that it couldn't see. While the horse was furiously fighting the discomfort of the bit in its mouth, they threw a saddle onto it, and cinched the girth tight. Then they lowered the cowboy onto the saddle, and the ranch hands scattered as the horse exploded with fury. The cowboy's job was to hang onto the horse until he broke its spirit, and the horse lost its willpower to resist. Eventually the horse learns that it can't throw off the rider, and exhausted, it submits. It's a brutal process, but it's the way riders and trainers have done it for thousands of years.

Thoroughbred horse trainers must break horses differently, because the horse is much too valuable to risk injuring it in such a dangerous procedure. So thoroughbred horse trainers have traditionally broken their horses in a more humane manner, but it's far more time consuming. After the horse has become used to wearing a halter, the trainer gradually eases a break-in bit into its mouth, and ties it loosely to the halter. This special bit has small keys that hang down into the horse's mouth to distract it. The horse starts to play with the keys in its mouth, just as a baby enjoys chewing on a toy. In a few days they attach a single rope to the halter, and take the horse to a circular exercise ring, where they encourage it to run around the circle, with the trainer in the middle. Then they place a blanket on the horse's back, and finally a light saddle, but still don't try to mount it. After a few days of this, they substitute a bridle and bit for the halter and break-in bit, and attach two long training ropes. Then they start a process that may take two weeks or more. The trainer walks behind the horse and teaches it to respond to the movement of the reins. With patience, the horse will learn to turn left and right on command, and then learn to respond to a flick of the reins to go forward, and a tug to stop and go backward. The objective is to get the horse to learn to do figure of eight patterns on command, and to go backward and forward. If the horse resists a command, the trainer forces it to obey by hitting it with a whip. Eventually most horses will respond by learning to avoid the punishment, but some are such rebels that they never learn, and can't be raced. When the horse has learned to obey commands, the rider mounts the horse and continues to force the horse to obey, by using his whip and spurs. The method has several drawbacks. It takes many weeks and it doesn't always work, which leaves you with a very expensive horse that is only good for breeding. Also, it is inhuman. Not as violent as the cowboy forcing a horse to submit, but they're still trying to break the horse's willpower.

Monty Roberts has designed a method of breaking, or *starting* a horse as he prefers to call it, which takes only half an hour—not weeks. It always works, and is completely humane. He bases it on principles that we can easily transfer to our own development, or to influence the behavior of the people around us. It will work well if you use it to train employees. It could also solve many of humanity's problems.

That's the power of the behavior-training program that Monty Roberts has developed. He can accomplish a major behavior change in half an hour that takes other trainers weeks to accomplish.

What if you could shorten your learning curve to such an extent? What couldn't you accomplish? What if you could train your employees to change their behavior in minutes instead of weeks? Think how their lives and accomplishments could evolve into greatness.

The two main principles of Robert's method are that the horse must take responsibility for its own actions, and that it must pay the price for its failings. Although I'd heard great things about the method, I admit being very skeptical as Pat led me to the training ring for the demonstration. She told me that within 30 minutes, I would see a rider mount and gently ride a horse that had never had a saddle on its back or a bit in its mouth. She stressed that it works because the horse wants it to happen, not because it submits unwillingly. How was this possible? The top trainers in the world take weeks to get a horse broken, and then can't be sure it will work.

We climbed to the observation deck above the training ring, and I noted the time on the clock on the far wall as they led in a three-year-old mare. It was exactly six o'clock. "Roger, I assure you that this horse has never had a bridle or a saddle on it before," Pat whispered. The ring is fifty feet across, with a circular wall eight feet high all the way around it. We stood on a platform looking over the wall into the ring below. I didn't notice the door set into the side of the wall until it swung open and a groom lead in a beautiful bay horse that I judged to be about sixteen hands. Its lines were exquisite and its coat gleamed with good health. The trainer walked to the middle of the dirt ring and put down a bridle, saddle and blanket. The groom left shutting the door tight.

At first the horse just glared at the trainer, because it didn't know what to make of this new situation. The trainer carried a long nylon sash with him, which he eventually flicked behind the horse without touching it. This caused the horse to start running around the ring, which it did ten or twelve times before it began to tire, finally stopping to take another look at the trainer. Pat explained to me, "If the horse doesn't move toward him, he'll make it go back to work."

Soon it became apparent that the horse only wanted to look at the trainer, not approach him. So, with a flick of the sash, he started it running again. After a few revolutions, it became tired or bored, and stopped. Again it didn't approach the trainer and he encouraged it to start running again. The third time it stopped, however, it took a tentative step toward the trainer.

"It's deciding that approaching the trainer might be more interesting than what it's doing now," Pat explained.

As the horse took a second tentative step toward him, the trainer slowly turned his back to the horse, but tilted his head so that he could see what was going on. The horse almost touched the trainer with its nose, but not quite.

"Looks like he's not ready to join yet," Pat told me. "Almost, but not quite."

With a flick of the wrist, the trainer sent the horse back to running around the ring. The next time it stopped, however, the horse did *join* with the trainer, who slowly turned around and stroked its head.

"We won't know that the horse has joined until the trainer is able to pick up each of its feet," Pat told me. The first time he tried that the horse resisted and he sent it back to work, but the second time she seemed eager to have trainer stroke her flanks, withers and legs and pick up her feet.

"Is it true that Queen Elizabeth wanted to learn this method?" I asked Pat.

"Yes it is," she told me. "She heard about it and sent Sir John Miller over to investigate. Then he invited Monty and me to visit Windsor Castle and show the method to the Queen. When you come up to the house for dinner, I'll show you the pictures."

Now the trainer was easing a bridle over the horse's head and inserting a bit into its mouth. Pat told me that it was a rubber bit, so it was more comfortable than a break-in bit. If the horse had resisted, the trainer would have sent it back to running around the ring, but it didn't object. I glanced at the clock, which showed that only fifteen minutes had passed. The trainer attached long training reins to the bit, and started to work the horse around the ring. Every few minutes, he would stop the horse, and have it reverse its direction.

Pat explained, "In America, all the race tracks are counter-clockwise, but in Europe they go both ways, so we train them to lead with either foot."

Soon he put a blanket on the horse's back and finally he cinched on a saddle. At each step, he gave the horse the choice of going ahead or returning to running around the ring. The willingness to go ahead appeared to be because the horse was choosing to do so, not being forced to do so. Soon the groom brought the trainer a hard hat, and after the trainer crossed himself, the groom helped him up onto the horse so that his stomach lay across the horse's back. Once the horse became used to the weight, he swung up to sit in the saddle and put his feet in the stirrups. The horse appeared startled, but not distressed. Remarkably, he was able to ride the horse around the ring, reverse its direction several times, and make it go backward and forward on command. The clock showed 6:34. In 34 minutes, without once punishing the horse, they had accomplished what normally takes weeks of patient work. Also Pat assured me that this method is always successful.

I wouldn't blame you for a moment if you're now thinking, "This guy's talking about training horses, for crying out loud! What do I need this for?" But don't leave me now! This is important. This is not about training horses, or any other animal. However, what if we could apply this to training other people, and ourselves? I knew that Pat and Monty Roberts had given me the answer to developing incredible self-discipline. I knew also that they had given me the answer to getting anyone else to willingly do what we want them to do.

Think about how we normally go about developing the discipline to get something done. Let's say we want to quit smoking, lose weight, or complete a tough assignment. Don't we normally beat up on ourselves? We try to quit smoking and we can't make it, so our self-talk gets downright masochistic. "Why don't you just admit you're hooked, and you're helpless to control yourself?" Or we look at ourselves in the mirror, see how much weight we've put on, and think, "Oh that's disgusting! How can anybody bear to be seen with me?" Or we're burning the midnight oil trying to complete a project for a major meeting in the morning, and our self-talk says, "Why can't I understand this stuff? I must be a real idiot. Why am I always biting off more than I can chew?" Isn't our self-talk vicious! Would you let anyone else talk to you that way?

What if instead, we gave ourselves choices, the way that Pat and Monty Roberts give their horses choices? That way the smoker says, "By choosing not to smoke for the next hour, I am letting my lungs start to rejuvenate." The overweight person, instead of denying him or herself food says, "I am choosing to eat this apple rather than that piece of pizza, because I know how much my body will appreciate what I've done." The person who's struggling with a project can say to themselves, "I can quit anytime I want and suffer the consequences, but I'm choosing to stay with this. Then tomorrow I'll reward myself by stopping by the clothing store to pick out something really great to wear to the party this weekend."

Look at the way we normally attempt to control other people. "Be home by ten or you're grounded," we tell our children. "Do this right or you're in trouble," we imply to our employees. "Show up late for work one more time and I'll fire you." What if instead, we substituted the Robert's method of letting the child or employee choose between doing things right and getting rewarded, or doing things wrong and have the rewards withheld?

Behavioral psychology has been controversial. Few people want to see human beings manipulated like animals, nor do they want people telling them they have no free choice. What I was seeing at Flag-is-Up Farms however was just the opposite. The trainer wasn't manipulating the horse, because the horse was always able to choose its behavior.

Let's move on to chapter five now and I'll show you how most of the highly touted management techniques of the last few years have really been techniques in behavior shaping.

Chapter Five

The Principles of
Behavior Shaping

ost authors of the highly touted management tools of recent years based them on behavioral psychology.

In his book *In Search of Excellence*, Tom Peters stressed that top managers believe in "Management by walking around." Get out of your chair and wander around. John Doyle, research and development executive at Hewlett-Packard said, "If you don't constantly monitor people, not only will they wander off track but also they will begin to believe you weren't serious about the plan in the first place." When Ed Carlson took over at United Airlines as they were losing $50 million a year, he didn't spend much time in the corporate office trying to come up with a grand strategy to solve their problems. He immediately started getting on planes and travelling 200,000 miles a year just to be close to the employees. These top executives would probably deny that they were using behavioral psychology on their people. However, they were certainly using some fundamental principles of behavior shaping such as, constant reinforcement of behavior when it is happening. A pat on the back when the employee performs well is more valuable than an elaborate letter sent two weeks later. However, to reinforce behavior as it is happening you have to be there—you can't just hear about it through the company grapevine. Another fundamental of behavior shaping is that you must wait until the behavior occurs, because you cannot reinforce behavior that's not happening. To do that, you have to be out in the field, not behind your desk.

In their book *The One Minute Manager,* Ken Blanchard and Spencer Johnson told us to, "Catch someone doing something right." Again, this is at the core of behavior shaping. You must reinforce the behavior as it is happening.

In my friend Michael LeBoeuf's book *GMP: The Greatest Management Principle* he stressed that, "The things that get rewarded get done." That is of course rule one of behavioral psychology. He also stresses that behavior is a product of its consequences, not its antecedents. I will talk more about that later. Michael's book was a best seller because it stressed how far American business has moved away from what we all know to be the best way to treat people. For example, the automakers want their assembly line workers to be long time loyal employees. Yet they reward them on a short-term basis, and lay them off the moment business slows down. Corporate suppliers want to build long-term relationships with their customers, and yet they reward their salespeople only for the sales they make on a month-to-month basis. Manufacturers want quality but reward workers for quantity, with only minimum standards for quality.

Management by walking around. Catch people doing something right. The things that get rewarded get done. The authors based all of these management principles on behavioral psychology, not cognitive psychology.

Behavioral psychology is the most effective way to change your life, and it's the most effective way to influence the people around you. The problem is that it is a branch of psychology that cognitive thinkers have maligned in recent years.

The first problem is that the behavioral psychologists did much of their initial research on animals, and naturally, we have an aversion to treating human beings in the same way that we treat animals.

The second problem is that some people see behavioral psychology as taking away our ability to choose. They say that past reinforcements have conditioned us so much, that we can never break that cycle. That may be true with animals. My golden retriever shakes hands with me instinctively because his trainer conditioned him to do it when he was a puppy. However, we are not animals. Human beings can always change. It's a shame that so many pop psychologists jumped in and started messing around with behavioral psychology, because underneath all the hype is a very effective way of changing the way we behave. It is also the key to understanding and influencing other people.

In this country, Burrhus F. Skinner is the best known name in behavioral psychology. Skinner started his remarkable career in psychology because of a chance incident. It fascinates me how our lives can completely turn on a chance incident. In my case, it was a postcard from someone with whom I'd attended the London School of Photography. The postcard was from the Virgin Islands and he told me about his job as a ship's photographer. Had he not sent me the postcard, I would not have followed in his footsteps. I wouldn't have traveled the world, or met my wife, or come to America. Moreover, we weren't even close friends. I'm sure he thought twice before spending the few pennies in postage that changed my life.

The chance event that changed Skinner's life was reading an article in the New York Times Magazine. He had intended to become a writer, but was disappointed in the sales of his first book *A Digest of Decisions of the Anthracite Board of Conciliation*, which his father, an attorney for the Hudson Coal Company, had commissioned. It apparently didn't occur to Burrhus that even Ernest Hemingway couldn't have written a best seller with a title like that! Frustrated, he became interested in how people think, and psychology began to fascinate him. Just as he was deciding whether to continue writing books or go into psychology, he read an H. G. Wells' article. The Times had asked Wells to comment on the ongoing feud between George Bernard Shaw and the Russian scientist Ivan Pavlov. Does the name Pavlov ring a bell with you? It must have really rung a bell with Shaw because he called him a scoundrel who would boil babies just to see what happened. H. G. Wells, who had his own reasons for disliking Shaw, admitted that it was hard to compare the work of the two great men. However if they were both drowning and he could only save one, he wouldn't hesitate for a moment to throw the life belt to Pavlov. "What good is Shaw? He's only a playwright," he wrote. "Pavlov is a star who lights the world." That was all that it took for Skinner to change careers from writing to psychology, although he soon found himself disagreeing with Pavlov. The Russian scientist believed that people's behavior is a direct response to stimulus. You ring a bell and the dog's mouth starts to water. Skinner believed that reinforcement for past behavior causes us to do what we do. Had Pavlov not fed the dog after ringing the bell in the past, it wouldn't be thinking of food.

Although he was a brilliant man who changed the way we think, Skinner seemed to luxuriate in controversy. Later he wrote a bestselling book *Beyond Freedom and Dignity* that in part argued that the freedom granted us by our constitution could be self destructive. Not the kind of stuff that wins you an enthusiastic following. That kind of publicity didn't help the cause of behavioral psychology any more than his invention of an Air-Crib, which he claimed was the perfect environment for babies during their first two years. He meant it to be nothing more than that—a hygienic, temperature controlled environment that was healthy for the baby and convenient for the mother. However, the public misunderstood him, thinking he had created a human version of the famous Skinner Box that he used in experiments to prove how rats responded to reinforcement. It led to persistent rumors that Skinner's two daughters grew up insane, which is untrue. They grew up to become well-adjusted and successful adults. Debra is an artist who lives in London, and Julie is an educational psychologist in West Virginia.

Let's set aside all the controversy about Skinner, and accept a basic belief of behavioral psychology: that if you reinforce behavior it will be repeated. And if you reinforce your own behavior, you will do it again. Let me tell you more about reinforcing behavior. Remember I told you about the A-B-Cs of behavior? Antecedents, Behavior, and Consequences. When the consequence (what happens following a behavior) makes behavior more likely to happen again, the consequence has reinforced the behavior. Let's say that Harry, the town barber, closes up his shop early and goes fishing on his way home. If Harry catches a fish at the lake, it reinforces the behavior, and makes it more likely to happen again.

If Harry doesn't catch a fish and then his wife yells at him for not coming straight home, the behavior of closing the barbershop to go fishing is weakened. It's less likely to happen again.

Some consequences reinforce behavior, while others weaken it. A positive reinforcer is a consequence that strengthens behavior by its *presence*. That is, a positive reinforcer is anything that when added to a situation, makes the preceding behavior more likely to happen again. When Harry catches the fish, it positively reinforces his behavior.

A positive reinforcer is anything desirable, occurring with an act of behavior. Sounds easy, right? But there's a great deal of meat in that sentence. *A positive reinforcer is anything desirable, occurring with an act of behavior.* There are two major points there. First, someone must think it's desirable, so it's a very personal thing. Pat a small boy on the head and he's likely to go back to his coloring book with renewed enthusiasm. Pat a grown up on the head and she is liable to swat your hand away.

In business then, you must tailor the reinforcement to the individual person. Your sales representative in Texas may really value the call you make to congratulate her on the big sale she made. Your New Jersey sales rep may think it's incredibly manipulative or condescending.

One day I mentioned to my daughter Julia that my 30th anniversary in this country would be coming up in a few weeks. She knew how much it meant to me to celebrate the 30th anniversary of the day they stamped my immigration papers in New York City, and let me into this country. She went to great lengths to arrange a surprise celebration for me. The problem is that I don't like surprises. She had given me some clues about what it would be, telling me that it would start at noon and would take anywhere from an hour to twelve hours, depending on how I reacted. She said that it was in Southern California and it was something I'd told her I wanted to do, but had never done. As the day approached, I was beginning to get frantic because however much I racked my brains, I couldn't figure out what it might be. The day before the anniversary, I couldn't take it anymore. I said, "Julia, I appreciate what you've done, but why does it have to be a surprise? You may like surprises, but I don't."

She told me that she had arranged a lunch party at Club 33, which is one of the most exclusive and unusual private clubs in the country. Exclusive because they limit the membership—to get accepted you have to put your name on the list and wait for somebody to die. Unusual because it's located inside Disneyland and very few people know it exists. There's a small lane of stores in New Orleans Square that have street numbers over the doors. Number 33 is a plain door with a buzzer, but no sign. If you're a member or a guest of a member, and have a reservation, you press the buzzer and announce your name. This gets you into a beautifully paneled entry lobby with a brass cage elevator that takes you up to the dining room.

Julia didn't know a member, but she had a friend who knew a member, and she had to use all of her considerable persuasion powers to pull this together. We had a great time although she stayed miffed that I hadn't let it be a surprise. I tell this only to illustrate how careful you have to be when deciding what you think the other person will see as a reinforcer.

Not only is reinforcement a personal thing, but it's also a relative thing, meaning that depending on what's going on at the time it may or may not be a reinforcement. The horse at Flag-is-Up Farms only chose to join with its trainer when it became a more appealing choice than continuing to run around the ring. A drink of water would be a powerful reinforcement in the desert, but not in a rainstorm. A compliment may not mean a thing to someone who's walking off stage with an Oscar in her hands, but it may mean everything to the salesperson whose wife walked out on him last night. It's not only different strokes for different folks, it's different chimes for different times. Reinforcement is both a personal thing and a relative thing. It's effective only in light of the person with whom you're dealing, and what's going on at the time.

Let's look again at that description of positive reinforcement. *A positive reinforcer is something desirable, occurring with an act of behavior.* The second key is that the reinforcement must take place at the time of the behavior, or close enough so that the other person makes the connection, *without having to think about it.* If your sales person is thinking, "I wonder if he's being pleasant to me because of the way I handled the Johnson account?" there's no way you can describe your act of being pleasant as a positive reinforcer. You're not clear on the concept yet if your wife is thinking, "Did he bring me flowers because I cooked such a great dinner, or because the louse is feeling guilty about something?"

You're thinking, what's the big problem? I'll just say to her as I give her the flowers, "Honey, these are for cooking such a great dinner last night." Well, that's an improvement, but you're asking her to make a conscious effort to connect the two. She will probably think of that as manipulative. Far more effective would be a hug or a word of appreciation at the time that she served you the meal.

Remember I told you about the phrase in *The One Minute Manager* "catch someone doing something right"? Assuming the person enjoys praise, you have positively reinforced their behavior at the time it is taking place. Yes, you have strengthened his behavior, but a lot more is going on here. Implicit in the advice to "catch someone doing something right" is the idea that you're ignoring them when they do something wrong, and that's an important point.

Let's say you're the supervisor in a lawn mower factory. You're training a new employee to stamp out the cowling that goes over the blade. Wearing heavy gloves, he works a huge press in the middle of a noisy, dirty factory floor. He reaches over to his right and pulls a piece of metal into the jaws of the stamping machine. As he hits the foot switch, the top half of the machine slams down with a loud hiss, stamping out the shape of the cowling. Then the top half rises and he reaches in, takes the cowling, and places it on the stack to the left. Then he repeats the operation all day long, eight hours a day, five days a week.

If he's hitting the foot switch before he takes his hands out from the press, forget behavior shaping or catching him doing something right. You have to stop him before his hands and the lawn mower become one. On less critical matters though, you ignore the mistakes and reinforce the good things. If the stack of cowlings is a little sloppy, don't worry about it. Wait until he puts one on neatly, and mention how well he did it. If his rhythm is a little off, don't say anything until it improves, and then compliment him. A fundamental rule of behavior shaping is this: *you cannot reinforce behavior that is not occurring.* You must wait for it to occur, and then praise it.

When my son John trained my puppy Buddy to sit, it wouldn't make any sense for him to yell "sit" until he did it. With a handful of dog food, he had to wait until Buddy happened to sit. Then he would say, "sit" and give him a tidbit of food. The next time Buddy sat, he repeated the reward and the instruction. Within fifteen minutes, Buddy had figured out that if he sat, he would get some food. At this early point in his training, the command word is immaterial. He is only connecting the act of sitting with the reward. However, by spending only fifteen minutes a day doing this, John was gradually able to substitute the command word for the food. Then the reward for sitting on command became a pat on the head, or an encouraging word. It's so simple and easy when you understand behavior shaping. Try forcing the dog to sit by pushing his rump down, and soon you'll give up in frustration and send him off to an expensive trainer. So the key is: wait until the behavior occurs, and then reinforce it. Catch people doing something right.

It's strange that most people think of behavior shaping as only taking place between two people, or a person and an animal. When you become more familiar with how it works, it becomes obvious that we're shaping our own behavior all the time.

Try consistently catching yourself doing something right. You don't have to be as vocal as Michael and Ted, but quietly praise yourself when you do something right. Of course, the way you do it will depend on your personality. If you're an effusive, outgoing character you might say to yourself, "You're terrific! I love you, love you, love you." If you're more low key (as I am), you might say, "You know you're really quite good at this, aren't you, old boy?"

Remember Harry the barber, who closes his shop early to go fishing? If catching the fish means that Harry won't go to bed hungry tonight or his wife won't nag him, that aspect of catching the fish is a negative reinforcer. By fishing, he removes the unpleasant consequence of going to bed hungry or having his wife yell at him for being a poor provider. Keep in mind that punishment is not negative reinforcement. They're different because punishment takes place after the act, so it can't affect the behavior because it has already taken place. Punishment can only hope to deter a repeat of the act. Later, I'll teach you why punishing someone is not an effective way of getting them to change their behavior. It's the reason our prisons are overflowing and crime continues to go up. Unless we give the punishment at the time of the behavior, which isn't desirable under our justice system, we can't call it negative reinforcement.

Once you understand how positive and negative reinforcers work, you can analyze your behavior and create reinforcers to give yourself the encouragement you need. Your actions and the level at which you perform them are directly dependent on the reinforcement you receive. Purely and simply, you do what you're reinforced for doing.

Here in chapter five, I've taught you how positively or negatively reinforcing behavior can shape not just our behavior, but also our lives. We can also use it to shape the behavior of those around us, which is just as essential to achieving our full potential. However, that's only the beginning. In chapter six, you'll learn about the vocabulary of behavior shaping, and the more subtle techniques that behavior shapers use. You'll see just how fascinating and effective this science can be.

Chapter Six

The Vocabulary
of Behavior Shaping

So that you can take full advantage of behavior shaping techniques, I'm going to teach you a new vocabulary for describing your behavior. You'll find the effort it takes to learn it is well worthwhile. Once you understand behavior shaping and what it can do for you, you'll gain greater control over every aspect of your life. Instead of feeling that things are just happening to you, you'll see that everything you do is part of a chain of antecedents, behaviors, and consequences that you can easily identify and which go logically from one to another. By choosing to make adjustments at the correct point in the chain, you will automatically change your behavior. Remember that the only way you're going to become all you can become is to change what you're doing. Sure, changing the way you think is important, but unless it leads to changing the way you behave, nothing's going to change for you.

Some of the terms I'm going to teach you will seem completely wrong until you take time to think about them and apply them to your behavior and the behavior of those around you. And the first principle I'm going to teach you is one that seems all wrong when you first hear it.

The first principle is that *behavior is a function of its consequences*. As I explained in chapter five, behavior doesn't happen in a vacuum. To analyze the behavior and the reason for it, you also have to consider what happened just before the behavior and just after the behavior. Do you remember which one is more important? What happens before or what happens after? I wouldn't blame you if you said that what happens *before* the behavior influences it more. Something happens and we react to it, so it seems obvious that behavior is a product of what has just happened. However, you'd be wrong. That's what Ivan Pavlov believed, but Burrhus Skinner proved him wrong. He taught us that behavior is a function of its consequences—that what happens after we do something is what controls our behavior, not what happens before.

Remember the horse-training story that I told you in chapter four? The horse could choose to join, or not join, with the trainer. If it chose to join, then the trainer would reward it with strokes and pats. If it chose not to join, the trainer would make it run around the ring again. The act of joining or not joining was the product of its consequences. It wasn't reacting to something that had happened previously. It was reacting to what it was learning would be the consequences of its actions. Understanding this point is important in learning how to shape our own behavior, and the behavior of others. We relish dieting if we know that it will lead to a desired loss of weight. What we hate doing is depriving ourselves when we're not sure it will work. When we're unsure of the consequences, we're far less motivated. Students don't have a problem studying hard if they know it's going to get them an "A." What de-motivates them are bell curves, where they know that even if they stay up all night, they may not get an "A," because other students could raise the average. Employees don't have a problem breaking their backs if they know it's going to get them that promotion. What they hate is working hard and not getting the rewards they expected.

Let me give you a scenario to illustrate the point that people's behavior is a product of the consequences. Laura is a receptionist at a company that manufactures cellular telephones. One day Tom, a customer who bought one of their telephones a month before, storms into the lobby. He's very angry because his telephone isn't working. He bangs it down in front of Laura and screams, "I want my money back on this piece of junk. It has never worked right since I got it!" At that moment Laura's boss Doris is walking through the lobby and waits to see what happens, thinking that she may have to step in and take care of the problem. To her delight, Laura does an excellent job in handling the customer. Laura gets Tom calmed down, and fetches him a cup of coffee—decaf of course, because she doesn't want him any more stimulated than he already is. Then she takes the telephone to the service department and has it fixed while he waits. Later Doris compliments Laura on the great job she did. Laura thanks her and promises to try even harder in the future.

In this scenario, we have three acts or behaviors taking place: Tom bringing in the telephone, Laura handling him well, and Doris complimenting Laura. What happened (the consequence) reinforced each of these behaviors. Tom got his telephone fixed, Laura got praised, and Doris got a commitment from Laura that she'd try even harder in the future. Remember the basic premise of behavior shaping: behavior that is reinforced is likely to be repeated. Let's say that next week Tom's telephone breaks down again. Because yelling at Laura last week got his telephone fixed quickly, he's likely to yell at her again this week. Because Laura got praised for handling him well last week, she's likely to handle him well again this week. Because Doris got reinforcement from Laura when she praised her last week, she's likely to praise her again this week. So this week, we have the three behaviors being repeated. Tom yells, Laura's helpful, and Doris praises.

I hope you've been paying attention, because here's the question: is Tom yelling because of what happened last week, or because of what he expects will happen this week? Is Laura being helpful because of what happened last week, or because she thinks she'll be praised again? Is Doris praising because of Laura's reaction last week, or because she has learned what Laura's future reaction will be?

The answer is that they're acting because of what they expect to happen, not because of what happened in the past. Behavior is a product of its consequences. We behave because of the consequences we have learned to expect. Harry closes up his barbershop and goes fishing because he expects to catch a fish, not because he caught a fish last time he went to the lake. He *expects* to catch a fish because he caught one last time, but what he expects to happen this week is what governs his behavior. In the language of behavior shaping, the response becomes the stimulus. The response (catching the fish the last time he went) becomes the stimulus that makes him want to go again. Understanding that consequences cause nearly all behavior, not antecedents, seems like a very remote and abstract thing, doesn't it? It seems interesting but hardly critical to our success. The truth is that this is the answer to why you do what you do, and why the people around you are doing what they're doing.

Let me illustrate this with a common occurrence in business. You're in management, and one of your employees complains that you never give them credit for all the things they do around the office. You think, "Wait a minute, Mark Twain said he could live for two months on a good compliment. It can't be that long since I said something nice to them, could it?" I'm sure you've had this happen to you, haven't you? If the employee understood behavior shaping, they would know that the way to get praised, is not to complain about the fact that it doesn't happen, but to reinforce it when it does. On those (apparently) rare occasions when you do praise them, they should respond with a big smile and say, "I really appreciate your mentioning that. It's going to make me work even harder in the future." That's what they should do. However, what they've probably been doing is responding with, "I'm just doing my job." Or with sarcasm, as in "Well, it sure is nice to hear a kind word once in a while." Or they've used it as an excuse to ask for a raise, or time off. None of these would be a positive reinforcer for you, would they?

Understand that behavior is a product of its consequences, and you'll know why your secretary is late so often, why your sales rep in Detroit hates filing sales reports, and why your children don't listen to you. You'll also know why *you* do the things that stop you from achieving all *you* could achieve in life.

To make behavior shaping easier to understand, I've been referring to reinforcers as something that happens to you, praise, or a reward, or somebody throwing you a dog biscuit if you happen to be a Pit Bull. We call these external reinforcers extrinsic. However, some of the most powerful reinforcers are not extrinsic, they're intrinsic, meaning within us. Intrinsic reinforcers are the pleasant or rewarding feelings that we get from the behavior. We hand a dollar to a homeless person and the good feeling we get from doing it makes it an intrinsic positive reinforcer to us. Intrinsic because it's within us, and a reinforcer because it makes us more likely to give away another buck the next time we see a homeless person. Unfortunately, it is both a positive and a negative reinforcer to the person getting the money. It is positive because they're being rewarded for their initiative in asking for money, and negative because the money helps one of their problems go away. Either way you look at it, it makes them more likely to ask for another handout, instead of finding their own solutions to their problems.

If all reinforcers were extrinsic, behavior shaping would be much easier to understand. The dolphin jumps out of the water and we toss it a fish. If the reward makes it more likely to jump out of the water again, we call tossing it the fish a reinforcer, and keep on doing it. With extrinsic reinforcers, we simply observe the action, and from the reaction see that it was a reinforcer.

Intrinsic reinforcers are not only harder to detect, they're also much more powerful. Researchers talk about intrinsic reinforcers being either primary or secondary. Primary intrinsic reinforcers are those needs or desires that come naturally to us, such as food, water, comfort, and avoiding fear and pain. Secondary intrinsic reinforcers are those that we learn, such as enjoyment of a smile, a good book or the sight of a golf ball flying 250 yards straight and true down the fairway.

I'd like to add another classification, which is what I call *core* intrinsic reinforcers. These are the ones that are so fundamental to what we value in life, that we can't even describe them. Isn't that a weird contradiction? We're unable to explain the things we value most in life,

Take the case of Krzysztof Wiecha a young Pole who bravely attempted to climb Mount Denali in Alaska. Formerly called Mount McKinley, the mountain is only 20,320 feet high, Denali is a killer mountain because of the bad weather that close to the Arctic Circle. The weather isn't the only reason, of course. Because you don't have to wait years for a permit to climb Denali, climbers from all over the world attempt it, and many of them are badly lacking in climbing skills and equipment. As many as 500 climbers may be on the mountain at one time during the summer climbing season. Krzysztof Wiecha was caught in one of the sudden and violent storms that make McKinley such a dangerous mountain. He was only 300 feet from the summit when it almost buried him. He dug a snow cave and survived alone for three nights of forty-below temperatures without food, water, or fuel for heat. Having climbed to 20,000 feet myself, I know how debilitating that altitude can be, even when the weather is good and you have adequate supplies.

On the fourth day the weather cleared and a rescue helicopter reached him just in time to save his life. In an Anchorage hospital, doctors had to amputate both of his frostbitten feet.

Why does he climb mountains? It is certainly not for extrinsic rewards. Over 7,000 climbers have reached the summit, so he wasn't going to make any headlines. Only climbers have been able to understand why people climb mountains anyway, and they would think him a fool for climbing alone and continuing to climb after he'd used up his supplies. The reinforcement he gets from climbing must be intrinsic. Something deep within himself makes it seem worthwhile.

How powerful can intrinsic rewards be? Unbelievably powerful, as I'm sure you'll agree, when I tell you that he is now back in Alaska, training to climb McKinley again. He's hoping to become the first footless man to reach the summit. Can you believe that?

I describe his climbing as a core intrinsic reinforcer because he's unable to explain why he climbs. The best he can do is to say that, "Up there, life is very clear." That's the way it is with the things that are valuable in your life. You can't explain why they're important to you. Try to tell me why you love your children. I bet you can't do it. You might start out by telling me some of their attributes. They're beautiful, or generous or smart. If I was to persist, and keep repeating, "Yes, but *why* do you love them?" you'd eventually have to say, "I don't know why, they're just so lovable." That's telling me that you love them because they're lovable. Core intrinsic values are impossible to explain. You just know instinctively that they're important to you. As Dave Barry said in his Miami Herald column, "If a woman has to choose between catching a fly ball and saving an infant's life, she will choose to save the infant's life without even considering if there are men on base."

Until he passed away at the age of 89 I had my hearing checked by Dr. Howard House, the founder of the House Ear Institute in Los Angeles. He is probably the world's premier hearing specialist. When I asked him why he still works every day, he really couldn't answer. When I pressed him, he joked, "Because I never took up golf." It's always that way with core intrinsic values. When someone really loves what he or she does, they can't tell you why they do it. And while they may joke about caring so much about what they do, that doesn't mean that they treat it lightly. Very often people are willing to die for their core intrinsic value because it's not only what they do, it's who they are. Take that away from them and life is not worth living. I think it's criminal to force someone to retire who loves their work, because you may be taking away their reason for living. As George Eastman, the founder of Kodak, said in his suicide note: "My work is done. Why wait?"

When I talk about reinforcers, don't think of them as only being extrinsic. Some of the most powerful reinforcers are intrinsic. They may be primary—such as your need for survival. Or secondary—meaning the things you've learned to love. Or they may be the most powerful motivator of all, what I call a core intrinsic value.

The next word in the vocabulary of behavior shaping is *extinguishing*. It's a remarkably simple and effective way to change anybody's behavior. Suppose you first learn a behavior because you're reinforced for it, and then as time passes, the rewards stop? Remember I told you about my dogs staring through the window? What would happen if I stopped reinforcing their behavior of looking through the window when they wanted to be fed? That's exactly what I ended up doing. It was so irritating to have them watching me eat whenever I sat down at the dining room table that I started to feed them randomly. I would continue to feed them twice a day, but never when they were looking through the window. Because previously I had positively reinforced their behavior of looking through the window, they kept trying it for a while. After only three days of ignoring the behavior, they quit trying. Simply by not feeding them at any time when they were looking through the window, I was quickly able to change their behavior. In behavior shaping terminology, I had extinguished their behavior.

Now let's take that a little further. Right now, they're not motivated because I'm feeding them. But what would happen if I stopped feeding them altogether? They would obviously try different things to see if anything would work. But what if nothing they did caused them to be fed? Would they start howling until I fed them? Would they eventually crash through the window and eat my dinner? Would they jump the fence and leave? You'd think the answer would be yes, but the answer is no! What happens is that they develop what I call *learned despair*. They eventually learn that *nothing* they do affects when they are fed, so they give up trying to do anything about it. What's even worse, they will not only give up trying to affect when they get fed, they give up trying to do anything at all. This is not because they become so weak from hunger that they can't move. Imagine that I could fit them up with an intravenous feeding bottle so that they got all the nutrients they needed, but they still felt hungry. They would be strong enough to attempt to change their situation and start getting fed again, but they would be helpless, because I had taught them that nothing they could do would change things.

It is also important to realize that even if I continued to feed them they could also develop learned despair. All I would have to do is be sure that I didn't feed them when they had done *anything* that they might interpret as causing themselves to be fed. If their feeding times were totally unrelated to their actions, soon all behavior designed to get fed would be extinguished, and they would be totally at my mercy for survival.

Learned despair is what's wrong with the inner cities of America. Learned despair is what keeps Linda Eagleson in the drive-by shooting war zone instead of moving out when her first son was killed. Unless her TV shows or anti-crime rallies have some affect soon, she's in deep danger of learned despair—which is believing that nothing she does can change things. Learned despair is what keeps families in poverty. They have learned that nothing they do can affect their condition. Mailing a welfare check to that person is a wonderful humanitarian gesture, but it's not going to make them try harder to help themselves, just the opposite. You only have to walk the streets of any major city to see learned despair in action. People don't sleep on sidewalks because they're responding to a particular situation; they are surrendering to the premise that nothing they do will make a difference.

If you visited Eastern Europe during the cold war, you saw entire countries that were victims of learned despair. I remember visiting Prague, Czechoslovakia when the Soviets still held it with an iron grip. I didn't realize until I went there that, under Communism, everybody works for the government—because there is no other employer. The man who sold me a newspaper on the street corner, the server who poured my coffee, and the man who drove my taxi were all government employees. Government control over the lives of the people was absolute, because without private enterprise, there was no alternate employer. And everyone had to work because it was impossible to become financially independent of the government—there was nothing to own and nothing in which to invest. Karl Marx said that he could sum up the theory of communism in one sentence: Abolish all private property. The Czechs were fudging on that a little because the government gave them permission to own a home and a car, but they couldn't own even a second home to rent out. Because the people were completely dependent on the government for everything, they had developed learned despair. You could see it in the faces of the people silently riding the subways. You could see it in the bored attitude of the workers. You could see it in the dejected body language of the people in the downtown streets. In pre-communist Czechoslovakia, hard work and enterprise were rewarded. When a behavior that was reinforced in the past is no longer reinforced, it will weaken. Ultimately, the behavior will extinguish altogether.

However, as soon as a few courageous people did speak out and tell the people they could take back control of their lives, that there was a way, a revolution took place. And I don't mean the revolution that toppled the government. I mean the revolution in the hearts and minds of the people.

Do all acts extinguish at the same rate, for everyone? No. There are many variables, including the expectations of the individual producing the behavior, and the schedule with which reinforcement vanishes.

Baseball players, for example, don't expect to get more than one hit for every three or four times at bat. Quite often, even good hitters will go to the plate a dozen times without reaching first base. Babe Ruth once suffered the humiliation of having three fastballs whiz by him before he had a chance to react. He turned to the umpire with a grin on his face and said, "Did *you* see any of those?" The umpire laughed and said no. "Neither did I," laughed the Babe, "but the last one *sounded* kinda high to me." Baseball players know that they have to fight the temptation to let their behavior extinguish. Because of this their motivation and willingness to keep trying will persist for a long time before it extinguishes, simply because they're accustomed to a highly intermittent reinforcement schedule.

Oscar winning producer and director Oliver Stone started out as a scriptwriter. For eleven years, he pounded out scripts without selling one of them. To keep doing something for eleven years without results, you really have to love doing it. Look how his love of writing carried him through some major disappointments. After submitting scripts to studios for eleven years, finally a producer hired him to write the script for *Midnight Express* and he won an Oscar for it. This suddenly made him a big player in Hollywood. Producers gave him approval to write and direct his first movie. However the horror movie, titled *The Hand*, was so bad that Hollywood ostracized him again. After self-exile in Paris where he became addicted to drugs, he returned to Hollywood for one last try. No one wanted to back him, so he had to mortgage his home to self-produce the brilliant movie *Salvador*. That made him a player again and he dug out some of the scripts he had written during the lean years. Learning from his bad experience with *The Hand*, he went back to the first rule of writing: write about what you know. *Platoon* was essentially the story of his experiences in Vietnam. He had volunteered because he was so distraught when his father died that he didn't know what to do. He *was* the Charlie Sheen character. He based *Wall Street* on his father's career as a Wall Street financier; and his drug problems in Paris inspired him to write the Jim Morrison biography *The Doors*.

In spite of his huge successes, his bad luck continued to haunt him. Four days before he was due to start filming *Born on the 4th of July* with Al Pacino in the lead, the German end of his financing collapsed. He was back to square one. Losing Al Pacino to other commitments, he had to recast with an unlikely Tom Cruise in the lead. Oliver Stone is truly someone who sees setbacks as Impermanent, Impersonal and Isolated. Much of that ability to keep going in the face of adversity comes from working at something you enjoy doing for the sake of doing it well.

What does this tell you? It tells you to find something you love to do so much that even if you didn't make any money, you'd still want to do it. That advice may sound very cerebral, but it's the heart of behavior shaping. By creating goals that are intrinsically rewarding, you reinforce your own behavior. When you're not dependent on reinforcement from other people, you put yourself in control of your destiny.

Let's move on to chapter seven where I'll teach you how to use behavior shaping to remove fear from your life.

Chapter Seven

Using Behavior Shaping
to Overcome Fear

In this chapter, I want to zero in on your fears and give you behavior-shaping tools to face them and overcome them. Fear is like a great fog that settles on your mind and stops you from getting where you want to go in life. When you sweep the fog away, your goals become crystal-clear and the pathway to them opens up before you.

In a famous skit from *Monty Python's Flying Circus*, a man politely knocks on an office door and then walks in. The man sitting behind the desk looks up and yells at him, "What do *you* want?"

"They told me outside . . . ," he meekly tries to explain.

The man behind the desk interrupts with, "Don't give me that, you snotty faced pile of parrot droppings!"

"What?"

"Shut your festering gob," he screams, "your type makes me puke."

"But I came in here for an argument," the newcomer protests.

Suddenly the man in the office turns ultra-polite. "Oh I'm so sorry. This is abuse. You're in the wrong room. You want 12A next door."

"I'm so sorry."

"No, not at all."

Although this is all a delicious piece of English silliness, the man behind the desk could have been a highly priced behavioral psychologist helping one of his patients to overcome the fear of being rejected. Behavior shapers call this process desensitization, and it's incredibly effective in treating your fears. The process involves exposing yourself to the fear in ever increasing amounts until your emotions are no longer affected by it. Ever wonder how a Gran Prix race driver can coolly throw himself into a tight turn at 150 miles per hour? It's because he's done it enough that he has desensitized his emotions to the fear. Ever wonder how a police officer can drive through an inner-city war zone night after night and not have a nervous breakdown? It's because he or she has become desensitized to the fear.

I know a man who's constantly asking women to dance, and is always being rejected. He comes back to the table and says, "I don't mind if they don't want to dance with me, but do they have to give me a long stare and say, 'You've got to be kidding.'" But he says it with a grin on his face. He really doesn't mind the rejection. Me? I'd die if that happened to me. That's because I'm so scared of asking strange girls to dance that I never do it. It's happened so much to him that he's desensitized his emotions to rejection.

This is another area where cognitive and behavioral psychologists disagree. The cognitive therapists would say, "Roger, lie down on the couch and let's see if we can find out why you're afraid to ask girls to dance." The behavior shaper would say, "Roger, go out tonight and ask six girls to dance. Start with the ones you don't like if you have to, but don't go home until you've asked six."

Albert Ellis, the father of Rational-Emotive Therapy, loves to tell the story of when he was a young man, and lived in the Bronx. Because of his fear of rejection, he had never in his life approached a strange woman. He gave himself the assignment of speaking to every young woman he saw during his daily visits to the Bronx Botanical Gardens. He didn't allow himself to be selective—he had to approach every young woman who was sitting on a bench by herself. At the end of a month he reviewed his scorecard. He had spoken to 130 women. Thirty of them got up and walked away. One hundred spoke to him, and one made a date, although she stood him up. What didn't happen to him was any one of the awful things that he had feared. Nobody called the police, nobody called him a pervert, and not one of them threw up because he approached them.

It was from this experience that he came to see how changing a person's behavior is more important, and much easier, than trying to change the way they think.

Into his late seventies, Albert Ellis still practiced psychotherapy in New York. A group of 800 psychotherapists once voted him the second most influential therapist in history, after Carl Rogers and ahead of Sigmund Freud.

The subject of fear is highly germane to behavior shaping. Remember our basic understanding about why people do what they do: a behavior that is reinforced will be repeated. Let's say that you're walking down a dark street late at night and you see two big mean looking men walking toward you. They're dressed in black leather biker outfits that are covered with chrome metal studs. Your stomach starts to knot up, and you begin to perspire. You feel fear spreading through you like warm syrup.

You have two choices. You can face the fear and walk toward them, or you can quickly turn down a side street to avoid them. Which would you do?

Since this is a thesis, I can tell you the result of either course of action. If you walk toward them, they will step aside and let you walk by without comment. If you turn down the side street, they won't follow you and you will never see them again. You might conclude that either choice was a good one. Not so! Turning down the side street was a big mistake.

Let's look at what happened in behavior shaping terms. Both courses of action were rewarded. In the first instance, you acted courageously, and your behavior was reinforced or rewarded. In the second case, you acted in a cowardly way, and your behavior was reinforced. And what does behavior shaping tell you? Right! That a behavior reinforced will be repeated. Faced with the same situation, you will act the same way again. So, what happens to you if you continually avoid your fears? You become so reinforced for doing so, that you become incapable of acting courageously.

The answer is obvious, isn't it? You must face your fears in such a way that you're reinforced for doing so. Otherwise, you get on a vicious cycle of reinforcing your cowardice.

Let's examine your fears and develop a plan for you to overcome them. I want you to listen to the following ten fears, and give me a score on a scale of one to ten, indicating how much they bother you, with ten meaning, "It terrifies me!" and one meaning, "Why would anybody be afraid of that?" Here are the ten fears:

- I'm afraid of losing all my money and having to spend the rest of my life in poverty.
- I'm afraid to demand more pay, because I might lose my job.
- I'm afraid to ask for the sale.
- I'm afraid of getting hurt, so I avoid sports like softball or football.
- I'm afraid of giving a speech.
- I'm afraid to speak up at a business meeting.
- I'm afraid to jump out of a plane without a parachute. OK! I was just checking to see if you

were paying attention! Make that afraid of sky diving, bungee jumping or running with the bulls in Pamplona.

- I'm afraid to ask someone out on a date.
- I'm afraid to argue with someone I love, because it might ruin our relationship.
- I'm afraid to change, because I'm comfortable with my life style now, and don't want to risk losing it.

Let's take just one of those and work through three different methods of overcoming the fear. I'll pick, "I'm afraid to ask for the sale." If you're not a salesperson, substitute any situation where you fear asking the other person for something.

The three methods I want to teach you are:
- Systematic desensitization
- Implosion therapy
- Self-confrontation

All of these methods are based on an underlying understanding: that you're afraid of something only because you have avoided it and therefore don't know that it can't hurt you. Let me explain that by telling you that I have a strong phobia of rats, which I picked up from reading George Orwell's *1984* as a child. I'd never seen a rat, so I certainly wasn't afraid of them before I read the scene where O'Brien tortured the hero Winston Smith by strapping a rat cage on his face. Ever since then, I've freaked out at the thought of rats.

Decades later, I remember having a bad experience with one in Hanoi. It was just after Vietnam finally opened its borders following the war. I was dating Katherine, whose big ambition in life was to visit Angkor Wat, the huge temple in Cambodia that had been closed to tourists for 15 years because of the war. Afterward we visited Ho Chi Minh City and Hanoi, where we stayed at the Dan Chu Hotel in the heart of the city. It is just around the corner from the city jail, which was known as the Hanoi Hilton when our POWs were held there. Since we were among the first outsiders to visit Vietnam since the war, there were no tourist hotels yet and the Dan Chu was very run down. One evening we went down to the bar for a drink. Katherine suddenly said, "Roger, I just realized that I left my jewelry laid out in the room. Would you mind getting it?"

I climbed the three flights of stairs to our room, and as I opened the door, I could swear that I saw somebody duck behind the partition that separated the bedroom from the bathroom. I had this overpowering feeling that somebody was in there. Pulling together all my courage, I crept toward the back of the room, prepared to wrestle with the intruder, but nobody was there. Almost shaking with fear, I gathered up her jewelry, went back down to the bar, and told her what had happened. Katherine, who suspects that all Englishmen are eccentric, wrote it off to my wild imagination.

When we went back to the room after dinner, she gasped and yelled, "Roger, look at that!" Something had dragged a banana from a basket of fruit that we'd bought at the market, and left it half eaten in the middle of the floor. Just as she said that I looked up and saw this huge rat race across the wall and disappear into the crude electrical box in the corner. Perhaps it was my imagination, but it looked as though it was a foot long from nose to tail. I jumped up, slammed the electrical box shut, and wedged it tight with a wad of paper. We slept uneasily that night, and when we awoke the next morning, the door to the electrical box was open and the rest of the fruit was gone.

Rats are my big phobia, but the point is this: that was the closest I've ever been to a rat. I've never held one, and one has certainly never harmed me. All of my fear is imagined. It's that way with most phobias. Had I been forced to go into a laboratory, pick them up, and pet them, as scientists do, I would get over it. That I've always avoided them has only intensified my fear, because I've never done anything that would contradict my feelings. All the techniques for handling phobias involve bringing the sufferer in contact with the object of their fear. Let's take them one at a time.

First, systematic desensitization, which means devising a system where you mentally face the fear so many times that you numb your emotions to the point that the fear no longer affects you. The word desensitization originally referred to a medical procedure for allergy sufferers. A physician can inject someone who has hay fever, for example, with increasing doses of pollen until the patient is no longer affected by it. It works 80% of the time. Psychologists borrowed the principle and applied it to the treatment of fear. To do it you write out a list of ten consequences of the act that scare you. Your list should start out with the mildest fear and build up to your worst nightmare. If we take the fear of asking for the sale, your list might read like this:

10. The buyer might say no, and I'd feel that I lost the sale because my timing was off.

9. The buyer might say no, and I'd feel stupid that I'd asked.

8. The buyer might laugh at me for being too pushy.

7. The buyer might laugh at me and say, "You don't know much about selling, do you?"

6. The buyer might laugh and call his secretary in, and say to her, "I just wanted you to meet the dumbest salesperson we've had in here all year."

5. The buyer might throw me out of his office, yell at me never to come back, and slam the door. Then I'd have to walk out of his lobby with his secretary and all the other waiting salespeople laughing at me.

4. He might call my boss and they'd both laugh at me, and I'd be fired and never find another job in selling.

3. I'd be disgraced, and when my wife and children found out about it, they'd be so humiliated that they'd leave and never talk to me again.

2. At my next industry convention, everybody would know what a stupid thing I'd done, and the entire room, all ten thousand of them, would point at me and laugh.

1. Once the TV networks found out how dumb I've been, they'd ridicule me on the evening news and everybody in the world would know how stupid I am.

Having developed the list, here's how you use it. You must first develop a control scene in your mind. This might be a peaceful beach in Hawaii that you visited once, or a lake that you fished when you were a child. My favorite spot is a peaceful lake in the Sierra Nevada Mountains that I discovered on a backpacking trip. Once you're able to hold the control scene firmly in your mind, you imagine the first item on your list with as much intensity as you can drum up.

The first one on our list was, "The buyer might say no, and I'd feel that I lost the sale because my timing was off." Feel this and experience it. It's very important that you get beyond the cognitive stage of just thinking about it, and into the behavioral stage, where your body is experiencing all the emotions of actually being rejected by the buyer. As soon as you feel the anxiety building to an uncomfortable level, switch to your control scene. When the anxiety has subsided, go back to visualizing your fear. What you're doing is re-conditioning your body's responses to the event. Whereas in the past the stimulus of the event had elicited anxiety, you have now re-programmed your body to answer with the relaxation response. During your practice sessions, gradually work your way up the list until even the most anxiety provoking condition only makes you feel relaxed.

Sounds like game playing doesn't it? However, it is one of the most successful techniques ever devised by therapists to handle fear. What I've done is adapt a method that psychologists use to treat serious phobias. Imagine that my fear of rats developed into a serious phobia. Several times a week I dreamed of being attacked by rats, and I'm now afraid to go into my garage because I'm convinced rats are there. My therapist might put me into a deep state of relaxation and then show me increasingly scary slides of rats. As soon as I became alarmed, he would turn off the projector and help me relax again. After five or six sessions, I would become comfortable with the slides, and the therapist would place a rat in a cage on the far side of the room. After ten or twelve sessions like this, I should be able to pet the rat without any trauma.

You can also desensitize yourself in two other ways:

The first method therapists call flooding, and it involves repeated exposure to the event that disturbs you. A therapist would use it by vividly describing a scene that you find disturbing. Let's say that you're afraid of flying and you can't get past his description of walking down the jet way to the plane without breaking into a cold sweat. Your therapist would record that description on a closed loop CD and your assignment for the week would be to listen to it continuously. After you've listened to the description a couple of hundred times, you will have desensitized your emotions to it, and you'll be ready to move to the next level of anxiety.

The other method is to break the mental association that you have with the traumatic event. Let's say that you're the president of a television network. To spice things up at your annual management meeting in Vail, you hired a stripper to make a point about freedom of speech. A little bizarre, but that's the kind of thing for which you're known. Unfortunately, the owner of the network was in the room with the Secretary of Defense. Neither of them saw the humor. The owner lost his temper and fired you on the spot. Every time you think of it, you cringe. What you should do is change the mental association of this scene from unpleasantness to sheer farce. Imagine your boss in a clown suit, with a red nose and a mop of green hair. Circus music is playing in the background. Now run through in your mind what your boss said, re-associating it with the ludicrous scene of the circus clown. By the time you've done this half a dozen times, you'll find yourself smiling rather than cringing when you think of being bawled out. You'll still be unemployed, but you'll feel better.

The second therapy for handling fear is the implosion technique. I'm telling you about it because it's so relevant, but I must warn you not to try it yourself. It's so potent that it calls for the supervision of a therapist trained in the method.

Implosion theory calls for you to visualize your fear in such graphic detail and with such exaggerated intensity, that you can no longer sustain such anxiety, and your fears implode, or collapse.

Let's say that you have an extreme fear of walking down dark alleys. Your therapist would have you close your eyes while he told a story of you walking down a dark alley and all the horrible things that might happen to you. Rats and lice crawl all over your body, and strange monsters rip your clothes off. Assuming you don't care for that kind of thing, the anxiety increases to the point of overload. You don't have the convenience of the pleasant control scene to which you can retreat. The whole point is to build the anxiety to the point where your will to resist the fear breaks, and you surrender to the fear. The therapeutic part comes in when you realize that you survive your worst fears.

It sounds dangerous doesn't it? It's like taking a five year old who's terrified of water and throwing him into the pool or forcing someone with vertigo to walk across the Golden Gate Bridge. Yes, it can be dangerous, and if mishandled can make the phobia more intense. To avoid the danger, clinical psychologists use blood pressure monitors so they know how intensely the patient is reacting. This serves a second purpose also. Often what the patient says they're afraid of is not the real problem. For example, they may think they're afraid of flying, but what really scares them is the crowd of people at the airport and on the plane. By talking them through the experience as they monitor their blood pressure, the therapist can discover hidden phobias.

As you can imagine, implosion therapy is not something you want to try on your own. A trained therapist will stop the session if he or she feels it could be harmful.

The third technique for dealing with your fear is self-confrontation. It is not only a very effective way for you to wipe out your fears, its effects are long term, perhaps even permanent.

If you confront something about which you feel strongly, and find yourself questioning your beliefs, a fundamental change takes place. The word for conflicting thoughts or values is dissonance. Researcher Milton Rokeach explored self-confrontation in a unique experiment, in which he created the greatest amount of human dissonance he could imagine. He brought together three acute paranoid schizophrenics, each of whom believed he was Jesus Christ. (Please don't try this at home!) All three had been confined to state mental institutions for many years. For three years, he had these three men live and work together. This placed each of the men close to two others—both of whom thought that *they* were *he*. How would you feel about that? You know who you are, but now you have to deal with someone who contradicts everything you've ever believed, by claiming that he is you!

Milton Rokeach found out that something has to give when you're faced with such dissonance. What gives is your belief system. If you use self-confrontation to face your fears defiantly, you can permanently erase fear. That's the good news. The bad news is that you have to go out and do it.

Let's take a look at the tough fears on the list I gave you earlier, and see what we can do to confront them.

Number 1 is "I'm afraid of losing all my money and having to spend the rest of my life in poverty." What you must do is go try it! Go live on skid row for a weekend and see how it feels. Buy some old clothes at the thrift shop, don't take a shower for a couple of days, leave all your money home and take a bus down to the worst part of town. Panhandle a few people, rummage through a few garbage cans for food, and try living by your wits for forty-eight hours.

Let me tell you what will happen. For the first few hours, you'll think, "This is stupid! Why am I putting myself through this misery?" Then you'll realize, "Hey, this isn't so bad! I don't like it, but I can survive." Next, you'll realize that even if you really had lost everything, you could still make it. You could figure out some way to get yourself out of the mess you're in.

You'd also develop a social conscience and empathy for the people who really are homeless in this country.

Let's see how it works with fear number 7. "I'm afraid of sky diving, bungee jumping or running with the bulls in Pamplona." Go do it! Since I talked about parachute jumping in my program *Secrets of Power Performance*, I've had dozens of people emailed me or called me to say that it inspired them to do it also. All of them thought it was the scariest but greatest experience of their lives. To confront that great impostor fear and defy it, changes you as nothing else can.

I also did a 250-foot bungee jump, an activity that highlights our two biggest fears. As you know, we only have two instinctive fears—the fear of falling and the fear of loud noises. Those two you're born with, and all the rest you have learned. So bungee jumping combines your two basic fears: the fear of falling and the fear of the loud noise you'll make when you splat on the ground if the rope breaks. No wonder the Maoris considered it a test of manhood! So to confront these fears I stood on the platform of a crane two hundred and fifty feet from the ground, with heavy elastic ropes tied to my ankles. My jumpmaster is telling me to let go of the rail, reach my hands out in front of me and dive off into space. If all goes well, I will free fall 100 feet before the slack in the rope is gone. Then I will fall another 100 feet before the rope is fully stretched. If the operator put on the right ropes for my weight, and if the platform isn't closer to the ground than they say it is, and if the rope doesn't disconnect or break, and if I don't swing into the side of the crane, I will stop just before I hit the ground.

As I stand on the platform, it occurs to me that this is far too many ifs for my taste. If only one of my concerns comes true, the story of my life will end within the next fifteen seconds. I don't want to die! Yes, I know death is a learned fear, but to me it's a big one.

Bungee jumping is a powerful experience because it all comes down to, "will you jump or won't you." Parachute jumping is different, because once you've jumped, you then have other things to worry about. You might have to use your reserve chute, and you might have to cut away the main chute if it gets tangled up in the plane or your reserve chute. You also have to guide yourself to the landing area, and worry about landing safely. None of this applies to bungee jumping. Apart from keeping your legs bent so you don't rip your spine apart, and resisting the temptation to grab the rope on the upward bounce, it all comes down to one thing: "Will I jump or won't I?"

What do jumpers think about as they stand on that platform? Perhaps some people worry about what other people will say if they chicken out. Perhaps some people do it so they can buy the tee shirt and brag about it in the bar. That wasn't it with me. It all came down to one thing: I said I was going to do it, so I'm going to do it. Commitment. Just like Bruno Kirby in the movie *City Slickers* bringing in the herd from the cattle drive. His friend screams through the storm, "Why are you risking your life to do this?"

"Because a cowboy doesn't desert his herd."

"You're not a cowboy; you're a sporting goods salesman."

"Not today," he replies. "Today I'm a cowboy." Commitment. Today I'm going to do something that's hard for me, just because I said I would do it.

Commitment, that's what it came down to with me. Common sense kept throwing objections at me: the rope will break; the wind will swing you into the crane; you'll injure your spine. And to each one I said, "Yes, I know that, but I said I would jump, so I'm going to jump." To me it was the ultimate confrontation between cognitive and behavioral thinking. When faced with my ultimate fear, can I override what I'm thinking, and still behave the way I want to behave?

The countdown comes. Five, four, three, two. This is the critical point. If I hesitate for an instant when I hear "one," I won't jump. The moment I hear the word I let go of the rail, and plunge forward. This is what committing suicide is like, I'm thinking. I can see the tower of the crane rushing past me at incredible speed. The ground is charging at me. "Oh, no, something's gone wrong," is my last thought before I feel the tug of the rope on my ankles. I stop, only a few feet from the ground. Then the elasticity in the rope fights for control and wins. I'm now catapulting upward with a feeling of complete weightlessness that only a few astronauts have experienced. I'm shooting back up toward the platform. I'm going to hit the platform on the rebound. Don't give me a lecture on physics; I know I'm going to hit it! Suddenly I'm suspended in air, neither going up or down. I reach for the rope instinctively—anything to hang onto—and then remember the instructions and pull my hands back. Then the downward plunge begins again. Again I'm plunging for the ground, but now something has changed. I no longer fear death. I have confronted the fear and broken the association in my mind. That's what self-confrontation is all about.

Behavior shapers say that all fear is like that. Because behavior that is reinforced will be repeated, when we avoid our fears instead of facing them, we reinforce the avoidance of fear. To overcome our fears, we must reverse that cycle. We must confront them, and see how rewarding that can be also. When we reinforce our behaving fearlessly, we reverse the cycle and begin to build our courage.

To be completely without fear is to self-actualize. In this state, we're happy, cheerful, confident, and we can make decisions quickly and confidently. We feel that we're doing the things we want to with our lives. Time passes quickly because we're so absorbed in what we're doing. That should be our quest—to create a world with no fear standing between our future and us.

Chapter Eight

Examining Ways to Change Other People's Behavior

Until now, we've looked at behavior shaping as a tool to get people to do what you want them to do. Now, I'm going to teach you eight ways to change the behavior of other people. You'll be able to use these techniques to get them to stop what they're doing now, and change to the way you want things done. If you have an employee who isn't getting the job done, a customer or supplier who's giving you fits, or a family member who's driving you up the wall, you'll learn how to use behavior shaping to change them.

The first four methods, the ones that we'll cover in this chapter, are negative. However, they are probably the way you are trying to change people currently. The last four, the ones that I'll teach you in the next chapter, are positive. They are the better ways to change people, and are the methods I want to you to use. However, first let's look at the way you are probably dealing with people now.

Negative Solution One: Elimination

That sounds like a gangster movie, doesn't it? It's Warren Beatty in *Bugsy* walking into the mob's gambling joint and killing the manager because he's been skimming the profits. No talk of rehabilitation, or "what will this do to employee morale?" or "how will we ever find a replacement?" Just pull out a gun and eliminate the offender. Gangsters call it rubbing out, the CIA calls it sanctioning, the state calls it executing, and Adolph Hitler called it the final solution. It's ruthless and barbaric, but in behavioral psychology terms, you and I do it all the time. We face a problem and, instead of taking the time to change the behavior, we remove the source of the problem.

Employers fire a worker, rather than use their skills to change the employee's behavior. A wife divorces her husband when it would have been a simple matter to use behavior-shaping methods to change his behavior. Parents give up on their children and throw them out of the house. It doesn't even have to be that severe. If you've ever walked away from an argument, or said to a child, "Just do as I say," you've been guilty of eliminating the person, rather than making an effort to shape his or her behavior.

All of these solutions to a problem are undeniably effective and to someone who hasn't learned behavior shaping it may seem to be the only solution. Although it may remove the immediate problem, it does nothing to change the behavior of the other person. An underlying principle of behavior shaping is that you cannot reinforce a behavior that is not occurring. You must reinforce behavior while it is happening. If you tie a dog to the tree, it can't run away. That's fine, because it does solve the problem temporarily. Just don't fool yourself into thinking that you're training it not to run away. As any dog owner knows, the moment you untie the rope or the dog figures out a way to get free, all you'll see is the north end of a dog going south, probably at high speed. If you'll think of the behavior shaping tools that I taught you in chapters four, five and six—you've really strengthened the behavior of running away. Tying the dog to the tree was a negative reinforcer of the running away behavior, right? When it runs away, it removes the discomfort of being tied to the tree, which reinforces the behavior of running away and makes it more likely to happen.

Throw a person in jail, and they're less likely to repeat the crime, right? Wrong! A staggering 80 percent of the people released from jail will return. Isn't that incredible? Then consider that it's probable that over 20 percent of them were in jail for crimes that they didn't intend to commit—before we put them in jail, they didn't have a proclivity to commit crime. If that's true, then prison increases the likelihood of the prisoners committing another crime. It doesn't decrease the chances. All you can say with certainty is that while they're in jail, they won't repeat the behavior.

Let's look at some other examples of eliminating the behavior when you could choose to shape it:

- Your son gets bad grades in college, so you refuse to pay for another semester.
- Golf frustrates you so you play less.
- The dog jumps up on the couch so you don't let it in the house anymore.
- Your daughter wants to move back in with you, and you refuse to let her. (When I was a real estate broker, it amazed me to find out how many older people would sell their house and move to a condominium because of this. They felt it was the only way they could force their children to find their own home.)
- The person you're dating talks too much so you find someone else.
- Your significant other doesn't like to dance, so you give up dancing.
- Your boss is mean to you, so you find another job. All of these are examples of eliminating a behavior that you could easily have shaped instead.

I'm not saying that you should *never* use this first option. In the movie *The Silence of the Lambs*, Anthony Hopkins won an Oscar for portraying the vicious killer Hannibal the Cannibal. This wasn't a person on whom

I'd care to try behavior shaping. Probably the only practical solution is to lock him up for life and even then don't turn your back on him. Similarly, if you're a rancher in Montana and a wolf is attacking your sheep, the only practical solution may be to pull your rifle off the gun rack and kill the wolf. And if you have twenty ranch hands building a fence and one of them is consistently goofing off, the practical solution may be to fire him, not take valuable time reshaping his behavior. You could do it of course, but it may not be practical.

So solution number one, eliminate the person, is always an option. It's easy to do, it always takes care of the problem, and circumstances may justify that method. Just don't fool yourself into thinking you're changing their behavior, because you're not.

Negative Solution Two: Extinction.

Extinction means avoiding reinforcing a behavior until it dies. Don't confuse it with extinction of the species. The person doesn't die, only their behavior dies. Think of it as you would a flashlight that you have left on. If you do nothing about it, eventually the light will extinguish. Of course, the flashlight didn't extinguish itself; it was your behavior of leaving it on that did the deed. This is what I did with my dogs when they peered through the window waiting to be fed. By being careful not to reinforce that behavior in any way, they quit doing it. All I had to do was to be sure that I didn't get up and feed them when they were at the window, even by accident.

Observe a mother in a supermarket with a small child. The little boy keeps picking up things and screaming, "Can I have this, mom, can I?" What can we deduce from this scene—beyond the fact that the child speaks English atrociously? We know that at some time in the past the child's mother or grandmother, or somebody, has reinforced the child's behavior by giving them something when they screamed for it. If the mother were now to ignore the child, the behavior would extinguish—it would go away. Wonderful theory, but very hard to put into practice, because of the way we would react if the mother ignored the child. We would all think, "For heaven's sake, woman, do something about that screaming brat!" Peer pressure bears down on the mother, and she picks up her son, immediately reinforcing his screaming behavior. The other problem is that the supermarket is not Burrhus Skinner's rat box. There are many other possible reinforcers, other than the possibility that the child may get the candy or cereal he wants. Just picking up the item may be its own reinforcement. Also, simply being the center of attention may be reinforcement, whether or not he gets what he wants. Extinguishing behavior is hard to do with people in the real world.

Negative Solution Three: Negative Reinforcement.

The major difference between negative reinforcement and punishment is that negative reinforcement occurs *during* rather than *after* the unwanted behavior. Therefore, the subject controls the negative reinforcement, and can learn to eliminate it by behaving differently.

Negative reinforcement is the best behavior modification method in a specific circumstance, which is when you run into deliberate, willful misbehavior. When you're sure that the individual knows exactly what he or she is doing and that your authority is being tested, you should respond with negative reinforcement—a frown, a stony silence, a sharp tone of voice—that continues as long as the subject's behavior persists.

The key to successful use of negative reinforcement is to end it as soon as you notice improvement. Otherwise, the subject has not learned that he or she can control your response. If you have an employee who is habitually surly and uncooperative, you can choose to act the same way yourself, but you must change your response as soon as the employee responds in the direction you want, even if they only make a slight improvement. With negative reinforcement, you want people to see your unpleasantness as a consequence of *their* actions and not as something that is originating with you.

Negative Solution Four: Punishment.

Let me stress again the difference between punishment and negative reinforcement. Punishment takes place after the behavior, whereas negative reinforcement must take place at the time of the behavior.

Punishment of employees can take the form of docking pay, criticizing in private or in public, or threats of one sort or another.

The biggest problem with punishment is that it doesn't really motivate the behavior you want. It just motivates avoidance of further punishment. The employee may not know what you want, and may not even care, because the desire to avoid punishment over-shadows all of his other considerations.

Punishment is most effective against unwanted behavior that you catch early, before they make it a habit. The destructive behavior should be unusual, the punishment should come as a shock, and it should occur soon after the behavior itself.

Delayed punishment is very ineffective both as a threat and as a reality, which I believe is a serious prob-lem in our criminal justice system. Moreover, the effect of punishment diminishes with repeated exposure, causes feelings of fear, anger, resistance, and even hate in both the giver and the receiver.

In a perverse way, punishment affects the behavior of the punisher more than it does the person being pun-ished. Let's say your high school son gets a speeding ticket and doesn't tell you about it until his court date comes up, when he can't hide it anymore. You punish him by taking away the car keys for two weeks, dock-ing the fine from his allowance, and making him mow the lawn. Since his behavior of speeding has already taken place, you can't negatively reinforce it, because it's too late for that. The most you can hope for is that the punishment acts as a deterrent on future behavior. But look how your son is reinforcing your behavior of punishing him. You're sitting in your air-conditioned living room, watching football on TV, and sipping a brew. Through the window, you can see your son huffing and puffing as he mows the lawn. You're thinking, "Boy I sure showed him, didn't I? It'll be a long time before he does that again. Yes, sir." Unknowingly, your son is doing a beautiful job of reinforcing your behavior of punishing him, making it far more likely that you will punish him again in the future. Although punishment is not a good way to shape behavior, when it does succeed in halting a behavior, the result is positive reinforcement for the person doing the punishing. Therefore, it motivates the punisher to discipline again. A better solution for both of you, and the driving public, is to reinforce an incompatible behavior, which in this case would be obeying the speed limit. I'll cover that in chapter nine.

The insidious thing about punishment is that it is self-escalating. What would you do if after you caught your son speeding, you punished him by taking away the car keys for two weeks, docking the fine from his allowance, and making him mow the lawn—but it didn't affect his behavior? Then a month later the police caught him speeding again. Would you be objective enough to think, "Well punishment didn't shape his behavior, so this time I'll try another approach? I'll try being nice to him." Is that what you'd think? I doubt it! You'd probably give him more of the same wouldn't you? This time you'd take the keys for a month, make him pay the larger fine and the increase in car insurance, and make him mow the lawn all summer. That's saying, "Punishment didn't work last time, but I'll *make* it work this time."

A key to understanding whether punishment will work is knowing that it is not the amount of punishment that works as a deterrent; it's the probability of being caught. During the Los Angeles riots in the spring of 1992, Mayor Bradley called in every available law enforcement officer in an attempt to take back the streets. It turned the freeways out of the city into racetracks. People who would normally drive no more than 10 miles over the speed limit were out there doing 100 miles an hour. In announcements that only aggravated the condition, radio stations were pleading with their listeners not to take advantage of the absence of the Highway Patrol. Remember that the penalty for that type of reckless driving was as great as ever, but the likelihood of being caught was way down. It's not the amount of the punishment but the probability of getting caught that is a deterrent. We could raise speeding tickets to $500 each, but it still wouldn't slow people down.

However, if we fitted every car with an automatic machine that charged the driver's credit card $5 for every minute he drove over 55 miles per hour, nobody would speed, because the punishment, although small, is certain. Incidentally, that's not as farfetched as it sounds. In Europe, trucks and buses are all fitted with a speed indicator. While the fine is not automatic yet, if police stop a driver, the officer will inspect the speed recorder, and fine him for all previous violations. It's very effective. That's why behavior shaping is so effective—it's a small amount of reinforcement consistently applied. Some employers have fallen into the trap of giving huge rewards to their people to motivate them. I've seen top sales producers get a Cadillac and a trip to Hong Kong. The problem with that is that each year you must increase the size of the reward in order for it to be effective. Behavior Shapers say that a small reinforcement applied consistently is just as effective.

In view of this, isn't it strange that punishment is humanity's favorite method of shaping behavior?

The biggest drawback with punishment is that it doesn't teach new behavior in a positive sense. The person being punished may learn what he or she shouldn't do, but seldom will learn anything with which to replace it. Along with punishment, there should always be some type of positive reinforcement to point the offender in a new direction.

Another problem with punishment is that it's most effective when first applied, and then it gradually loses its effect. As that happens, we must invent newer and stronger punishments, and there's no end to it. A few years ago, I went to Pamplona, Spain for the Festival of San Fermin, better known as the running of the bulls. Before the festival, I spent a delightful couple of days in nearby San Sebastian, one of the prettiest ocean side resorts in the world. Like a miniature Acapulco, it has an almost perfectly circular beach with just a narrow gap between the two headlands. At the old fort overlooking the bay, they were displaying medieval punishment systems. In those days, they didn't wonder if executing people was fair. It was more a matter of *how* they would execute people who broke the law. It's amazing how cruel they were. On display was a big wheel on an axle pole. They fixed one end of the axle loosely to the ground so that they could roll the wheel back and forth over the victim to execute him by crushing his bones. Also on display was a hanging cage that they placed on a tall pole at the side of highways. They put criminals inside the cramped cage until they died of exposure, either in the heat of summer or the cold of winter. They then left their bodies in the cage as a deterrent to other people who might be thinking of stealing something! No wonder Thomas Jefferson insisted on a prohibition against cruel and unusual punishment in the United States Constitution!

I'm not telling you all this to ruin your day. I'm making the point that the threat of punishment, however severe, doesn't change people's behavior very much. If it did, it would have eradicated crime in medieval times, and of course, it did not. Today we look at these torture instruments of three hundred years ago, and think, "How could anybody be so primitive in their thinking?" Perhaps three hundred years from today society will look at our penal methods and think, "How could they have been so primitive as to throw millions of people in jail the way they did at the end of the twentieth century? Couldn't they see that it wasn't doing much to change the level of crime?"

Although punishment usually means something that one person inflicts on another, in behavior shaping we also think of it as something we do to ourselves. Self-punishment is probably something you have attempted in shaping *your* behavior. Guilt, for example, is a form of self-punishment that surely causes more problems than it solves. Shame is another form of self-inflicted punishment. These emotions may have short-term success in influencing your behavior, but some people seem compelled to go overboard with them.

Researchers Watson and Tharp reported an example of a man who attempted to stop smoking by getting his wife to participate in a punishment program. The man was an avid gardener and had an extensive collection of rare flowers. He and his wife agreed that for every cigarette he smoked, she would destroy one of his prize-winning plants. Over the course of a week, the plan proved successful, in the sense that he didn't smoke any cigarettes. Instead, he prowled the garden and wondered which of the plants his wife was going to sacrifice. How would she kill it? Would it suffer? You can imagine the negative effect all this had on their relationship. At the end of the week he canceled the agreement and went back to smoking, but at least he no longer felt like throttling his wife.

Self-punishment can be helpful, but only under certain circumstances and when you use it with great care.

However, there are times, particularly when you're dealing with your own behavior, when punishment seems to be the only answer. For example, you may love to play golf so much that there's simply no positive reinforcer that can compare. You rack your brains trying to think of a reward to give yourself if you painted your kitchen this Saturday morning instead of playing golf with your buddies, and can't think of a thing. Playing golf *is* the ultimate reward for you. In that situation, positive reinforcement isn't viable, and some kind of self-punishment may be the only thing to keep you off the golf course. What kind of punishment should you use?

Researchers say that giving up something pleasant is more effective punishment than introducing something unpleasant. It's more effective to make a deal with yourself that you'll skip dinner at the country club Sunday night if you play golf, rather than saying that you'll not only spend Sunday painting the kitchen but will also clean out the garage. Furthermore, the loss should come out of bonus rewards, not customary ones. You're attempting to remove a premium, not create a penalty. If going to dinner at the country club on Sunday night is part of your regular routine, forcing yourself to skip it becomes a penalty, not the removal of an incentive. If dinner at the country club is a special treat to which you've been looking forward, then making a deal with yourself to forgo it if you break down and play golf, will be more effective.

At best, see self-punishment as a temporary, supplementary tactic for achieving carefully chosen objectives. I only suggest it with the following conditions:

- Remove something positive rather than adding something negative.
- Devise a plan that combines punishment with positive reinforcement.

- Use self-punishment as a temporary deterrent strategy, and as soon as you can switch to positive reinforcement, do so.

Finally, remember that many studies demonstrate that rewards and positive reinforcement are a far more effective way to shape your own behavior. Don't fall into the trap of slapping yourself when you should be patting yourself on the back.

In this chapter we've looked at the four negative ways to change other people's behavior:

1. Eliminate the offender, by firing them, divorcing them or in some other way getting them out of your life.

2. Extinguish the behavior by consistently failing to reinforce it.

3. Negatively reinforce it by withdrawing support, or in some way, disapproving of the behavior *as it is happening.*

4. Punish the behavior in the hope that it will act as a deterrent.

These are the four that I want you to stop doing, and instead substitute one of the four *positive* ways to change behavior that I'll cover in the next chapter.

Chapter Nine

4 Improved Ways to Change Other People's Behavior

I n the previous chapter, I taught you the four negative ways to change other people's behavior. In this chapter, I'll teach you four positive ways of dealing with problem behavior. They are definitely more effective, and I promise you that once you learn them and start applying them, you'll never go back to your old ways.

Positive Solution One: Condition people to react with an incompatible behavior.

It's impossible to react to a stimulus in two different ways at the same time. So if you train the other person to react in a way that's in conflict with the behavior you want to stop, then you can quickly extinguish it.

Let me give you an obvious example of shaping an incompatible behavior. You have a dog that likes to jump into your favorite chair the minute you get up. To cancel out the behavior you train it instead to lie in the corner by the television, using positive reinforcement. The dog can't be in two places at one time. So, by training it to lie in the corner, you have also trained it not to jump into your chair. Easy, right? But how does that apply to people?

I once worked with a telemarketer who was so afraid of rejection that she was afraid to ask for the order. She was great at prospecting but froze up when it came to asking for the sale. How could I train her in an incompatible behavior? What I did was make rejection the goal. For a week, I told her that I would give her a dollar for every time she was rejected. Suddenly her attitude went into reverse gear. Before, she was afraid of asking for the order because she saw the customer saying "no" as rejection. Now I was training her to see the customer's no as winning. The only way she could win now was to do something that she hadn't been doing before, which was *ask* for the order. See what happened there? Before, the behavior I wanted to eliminate was fear of rejection. By reinforcing the behavior of being rejected, I was training an incompatible behavior.

Now, to be rejected she had to ask for the order. Guess what happened? Of course! Some of the customers said "yes"! Once that started happening, she quickly learned how much commission she could earn by asking for the order. Obviously, this is a quick fix remedy. I wouldn't want to reward her on a long-term basis for customers who said "no," to the point where she was encouraging rejection.

Without realizing it, we often train ourselves in incompatible behaviors. We feel lonely, so we switch on the television. It's very hard to feel lonely if you're watching something that engrosses you—so although you're still alone, it changes your mood.

We feel miserable, so we go to the store and buy something. The feeling we get from spending money is incompatible with being miserable, so it changes our mood for a while.

Here's a helpful technique that employs shaping an incompatible behavior. Did you know that it's almost impossible to feel depressed when you're looking up? Tony Robbins taught me this. I've known Tony for about 30 years, so when we see each other, we joke about how it was when we were just getting started. Finally, I got around to taking Tony's famous fire walk. He'll take anyone and, in an evening, get them to overcome their fear of walking over a bed of burning coals. If you haven't done it yet, you're probably as skeptical as I was when I started the evening. At eight o'clock I was saying, "No way is anybody going to talk me into doing something that stupid." By ten o'clock, I was saying, "Well, I'll watch and see what happens, but I've bungee jumped and I've parachuted, so I don't need to prove how fearless I am." By midnight, I was saying to my son Dwight, "OK let's do it." One of the things that Tony teaches you is to look up as you walk down the bed of coals. At first, I thought it was because you'd freak out if you had to look at the glowing coals on which you were walking. However, that's not it at all. It's virtually impossible to feel fear or depression when you're looking up. That's why speakers like the audience to be looking up at us. We hate those auditoriums where we're in a pit and the audience is looking down at us. That's why the Greeks were so good at tragedies—in an amphitheater everyone is looking down at you, and it's very depressing for the audience.

Here's how I used it to handle a difficult problem. After 66 years of marriage to my father, my mother passed on to a glorious life in the next world. Dad was 89 when it happened, and I thought it was going to kill him. To compound the problem, he suffered acute short-term memory loss and often forgot that she had died, so I had to tell him about it again every time I saw him. It was particularly difficult for him when he would come to my home for lunch or dinner, because in the past he'd always come with mom. He wouldn't be there long before his eyes would start to mist over and he'd start talking about how much he missed her. Then I remembered what Tony Robbins had taught me about looking up. Every time I saw my father's eyes start to water, I would say to him, "Dad, can you see that airplane up there? What do you think it is?" If we were indoors I'd say, "Dad, do you know how they put that ceiling up there without any seams in it? How do they do that?" He would look up and completely forget that he was about to get depressed as he stared up and concentrated on answering my question.

Looking up is incompatible with depressing thoughts, so I was using behavior shaping to train him in an incompatible behavior.

Positive Solution Two: Put the behavior on cue.

In the simplest of terms, this means that to stop the other person doing something, you train them to do it only when you tell them to. Sounds manipulative, and of course it is, but sometimes it's a simple way to solve a troubling problem. Let's say that you're a nursery school teacher. Your job is to spend the day with thirty hyperactive four year olds. Their little bodies are so full of sugar coated cereal and candy that the energy has to go somewhere, or they'll explode. Doesn't that sound like fun? All day long, they're racing around the room yelling and screaming with excitement. Your behavioral challenge is to get them calmed down. If you were using reinforcement you would wait until they calmed down and then reinforce that behavior. The problem with that method is that they never all calm down at the same time.

This is a situation where you'd be better off to put the behavior on cue. You'd say, "OK children, now we're going to play a great game. Let's all get crazy together. Let's run around the room making as much noise as we possibly can! Do it when I say go, and stop when I raise both my hands like this." After the exercise is over you ask them, "How many of you thought that was fun? Raise your hands if you did. That's great! Everybody liked doing that. So tell you what, later this morning we'll do it again. So watch for my signal, and when I waive my hands like this, we'll all get crazy together." It's obvious what's going to happen isn't it? The children are going to wait until they get the cue from you before doing what they were doing randomly before.

I was visiting a client of mine whose offices were only a few blocks from Venice Beach California, the casual attitude capital of the world, and noticed that they were having a "dress-down" day. If you're not familiar with this California custom, a "dress-down" day is one day a week when management allows the employees to come to work in casual clothing. It has become so popular in California that it no longer alarms us to walk into a bank and find all the employees in blue jeans and T-shirts. I said to my client, "I see you're having a dress-down day. Friday is dress-down day at my company, and I hate it. It always seems to me that sloppy dress leads to a sloppy attitude toward work. Whenever I go to my office on a Friday, I feel that mentally they've already started the weekend."

"Roger," he said, "I tend to agree with you, but when I took over this company, every day was dress-down day. At least this way they only dress sloppily on Wednesdays, and it's a vast improvement."

I found his response fascinating. I knew this man well. If I had tried to sell this man on using behavioral shaping techniques on his employees, he would have had a fit. He would have said, "Roger, I'm not going to use that B. F. Skinner stuff on my employees, it's far too manipulative." And yet when he had a problem with his employee dress code, he solved it by putting the employees' behavior on cue. He had unknowingly used one of the subtlest behavioral shaping techniques in the book.

Remember when I told you about staying in the longhouse in Borneo? Enbadin, the chief of the longhouse, told me about a ritual that he uses to control the behavior of his people. When he feels that the behavior of his people is getting out of hand, he declares a "Devil Antu" or Festival. For two days everybody goes wild and sleeps with everyone else, to get the evil spirits out in the open. When the festival is over, everybody goes back to his or her normal behavior. Chief Enbadin had never heard of B. F. Skinner of course, but his ancestors had passed down the technique of putting behavior on cue. Many primitive societies recognize that within us all is the ability to behave in unacceptable ways, and they encourage people to get it out of their systems by declaring a day when that behavior is acceptable.

I have used "putting behavior on cue" many times at my company, and I don't mean by declaring a Devil Antu. Something disappointing happens, such as a big sale that falls through at the last moment. If I don't do something there is likely to be a black cloud of depression hanging over the office for the entire day. So, I put the depressed behavior on cue. I say, "OK this is a big setback for us, and we have every right to be upset, angry and depressed over it. But not forever. Let's all be upset for two minutes and then we can get back to work." So I look at my watch and say, "Go." Everybody starts moaning and groaning and the air turns blue with cuss words. When the two minutes are up, I say, "Stop! Time's up, let's forget about it now, and move on. I have $5 here for the first person who gets on the phone and bags a good solid lead." And it's all over. What could be simpler? Usually it doesn't even take two minutes, because we soon start thinking how stupid we all look moaning and groaning over the loss of one sale, and we all collapse in laughter.

Positive Solution Three: Reinforce the lack of the behavior.

This technique takes a little patience but it's a very pleasant and effective way to change people's behavior. Let's say that you have an assistant who is frequently five minutes late to work. You could choose to make an issue of it every time he comes in late, but think of all the negative issues that could raise:

- He may think you're nit-picking.
- He may find worrying about being punctual is so stressful that it takes him half an hour to become effective once he does get to work.
- He may feel that you're giving so much attention to when he shows up, that he starts thinking you judge his performance only on punctuality.
- The situation begins to irritate you out of all proportion to its true seriousness.

Instead I suggest you ignore the times when he's late and concentrate on praising the times when he's punctual. Behavioral psychologists call this reinforcing the lack of the behavior. It's amazing how you can change the atmosphere in your office just by taking that approach.

Let's examine the behavior of being late for a moment. How willful is the misbehavior? In other words, how conscious is your secretary that he's frequently late for work? At one end of the scale, he may be completely unaware that you consider him tardy. Perhaps on the way into the building he stops by the mail room to see if any faxes came in for you overnight. He considers that reaching the *mailroom* by 9 AM means that he's on time. It never occurs to him that you're upstairs fuming because you consider that getting to his *desk* at nine means being on time. At the other end of the scale, you have someone who is willfully misbehaving. They're doing it just to "get your goat." In the bar after work, they're saying to their buddies, "You should have seen my boss this morning; the veins were popping out of her head. I swear one day she's going to drop dead of a heart attack."

This technique works well at both ends of the misbehavior scale, but not so well on people who are in the middle. To the person who's unaware that they're displeasing you, reinforcing the lack of being late gives them a warm fuzzy when they get to their desk early. This is the way they would see it. They may never realize what you've done; they just know it feels good to be early to work.

To the person who is willfully misbehaving just to irritate you, it works well also, although it becomes a different technique when you do it then. By praising this person when he's on time, and not commenting when they're late, you're really removing his benefit for being late. Since being late no longer irritates you, it takes the fun out of it. Removing the benefit is the fourth positive way to handle problem behavior, and I'll cover that later in this chapter.

Reinforcing the lack of the undesirable behavior doesn't work as well with people who are in the middle of the scale, those who are occasionally late, and feel bad when they are. Not mentioning their tardiness may seem condescending. Praising them when they next come in on time can appear sarcastic.

At this point, you may well be thinking, "Why go to all this trouble? My assistant is being paid to be on time. If he's late I'm going to tell him to knock it off, and if he doesn't don't knock it off, I'm going to replace him. End of story." I hear you, but let me make a point about this. I'm not suggesting that if you're C.E.O. of a Fortune 500 company who's paying your assistant $100,000 a year that you have to coddle her. If she is that high on the feeding chain, she is expected to handle little things like showing up on time without any supervision from you. However not many of the people you'll work with during your career are that impressive. I think it's a real mark of maturity in a manager when you realize that you will have to get the job done mainly through employees who need this kind of behavior shaping.

Back in 1975, I was a personnel manager at a large department store in Torrance, California, just a mile from one of the best beaches in the State. I spent most of my time trying to bring the latest management techniques to our 35 department heads. I taught them all about "x" versus "y" management styles, the management grid, and assertive versus emotional personality styles. However, I knew that most of their sales clerks were college students. On any bright sunny Saturday in summer, they developed a strong tendency to call in sick and head for the beach. So, if the weather was great, we had to throw out all the grand management principles and have a victory celebration if they showed up for work at all!

Every new manager goes through the frustration of finding out that the people with whom he has to work are not half as skilled or motivated, as they are themselves. Mature managers realize that getting the job done means getting it done with the people who are available to you. So, a behavioral shaping technique like reinforcing the absence of poor behavior may seem childish to you. But it may be what you must do to get the job done.

Another thing that amazes me is how someone who instinctively knows how to get the best results from people in a recreational setting will do exactly the opposite when they're in a management position. When I speak to a corporation that is having their annual sales meeting or to an association having its convention, they often invite me to play golf with them in their tournament. By the time we play, I've learned a lot about how these executives run their companies. On the golf course, I get to see them in a different environment.

When people play golf together, they always praise the other player's good shots and ignore the bad shots. Furthermore, it's done in relationship to each player's level of ability. A low handicap golfer will only get praise for an exceptional shot. A duffer will get praise for making any kind of contact with the ball. Which is exactly the behavior technique that we're talking about here, isn't it? Ignore the poor behavior and praise the good. I usually give the executive high marks for behavior shaping when he's on the golf course. So, why is he such a nit-picking tyrant at work, when he is so good at behavior shaping on the golf course? At his company, his people say, "I never hear any praise from him. The only time he speaks to me is when I foul up." If he took what he instinctively knew to be effective behavior shaping on the golf course, and had enough confidence in it to apply it to his business, he could double his effectiveness.

As I said, reinforcing the lack of undesirable behavior takes patience—but it's a very pleasant and 98 effective way to change people's behavior.

Positive Solution Four: Remove the benefit for the undesirable behavior.

This is by far the most desirable method and is usually effective. Let me give you a problem and see if you can figure out how to change the behavior by removing the benefit. My friend Jack Harvey told me of an experience he had as a teenager working on a farm in England during the summer. He was one of ten workers whose job was to spread two tons of manure over a four-acre field. He was eager to do the work, but when he looked at the other nine workers, he knew they wanted do as little work as possible. How did he get them to do their fair share?

Let's examine the problem. The undesirable behavior is the laziness of the other workers. Question: What is the benefit for their lazy behavior? Answer: The less they do the easier their day will be. The solution Jack came up with was to remove any benefit to the lazy behavior. How would you do that?

Here's what Jack did. He got agreement from them that they would have the manure dropped off in ten equal piles. Each man's job was to spread their pile of manure, and as soon as they had done it, they were free to go home for the day. He had changed the undesirable behavior of laziness by removing any benefit for slacking off.

It sounds so common sense that it appears to be the obvious thing to do, doesn't it? But look at the way most businesses work:

- We want people to be productive but we pay them for the hours they work, not what they get done.
- We want executives to be team players and yet we set up an arena of intense competition for promotions.

- We want salespeople to be consultative in dealing with customers—to put the customers' interests first—and yet we pay them on straight commission.
- We want our salespeople to work as a team and yet we set up contests that glorify the top producers at the expense of humiliating those who sell less.

Let's look at ways that we can change people by removing the *benefit* of their undesirable behavior:

- Behavior: A mugger is threatening to shoot you. The way to remove the benefit: Give him your money.
- Behavior: Your son whines for candy when you take him to the market. The way to remove the benefit: Give him candy before you go into the store.
- Behavior: Your employees want to join a union. The way to remove the benefit: Give them the benefits they would have if they did join. The benefits may not have to be tangible, because they may need only an arena in which to gripe.
- Behavior: Your customers want sixty-day terms. The way to remove the benefit: Unless they're in serious financial trouble, give them the extended terms; but only if they trade off some other benefit, such as quantity discounts or expedited shipping.

- Behavior: Your employees are grumbling behind your back. The way to remove the benefit: Give them a forum for making their complaints heard.
- Behavior: Your secretary doesn't think that bringing you coffee is part of her job description. The way to remove the benefit: Make it optional. Chances are she won't mind doing it if she doesn't have to.

Although removing the benefit for the undesirable behavior is probably the best method, it is also the most challenging for the manager. It means that you make an accurate assessment of what is motivating the problem behavior. Let's say that you're a vice-president in charge of production at a bowling ball factory. You get complaints from some of the assembly line workers that a supervisor is making their life miserable by constantly bossing them around. This behavior shaping technique calls for you to remove the motivation for the behavior. The problem is to uncover the motivation. Does the supervisor want more power, so he bosses around his subordinates? Or is he really insecure and he needs reassurance?

Perhaps the head of the shipping department recommends replacing one of the office clerks because she's so slow at processing the shipping paperwork. You would prefer to shape her behavior because you feel she has the potential to become a top-notch employee. Before you can do that, you need to understand her motivation.

Does she simply want to put in her time and collect her check? Or does making a mistake terrify her because she fears losing her job? Before you can remove the motivation for the bad behavior, you have to understand their motivation. The key to doing that is to understand the four driving forces that I taught you in chapter two. Are they primarily an Acceptance person, or does a need for Competence drive them? Is Direction the moving force in their life, or is it the need to Control?

Once you understand the motivation, restructuring it can be straightforward. You can tell the power-hungry supervisor that you give promotions to the most democratic of supervisors, not the most autocratic. If insecurity is the problem, you may need to put greater emphasis on employee feedback as a way of evaluating his performance. The message you need to get across is that job security comes from having a team of employees who support him. You may need to tell the slow-moving shipping clerk that she can go home when the work's done, rather than having to stay until a set hour. However, if the problem is fear of making a mistake, then she may need reassurance that your back up system will catch any mistakes, and she's not going to be fired for it. If you can identify the underlying cause of a problem, you can eliminate the motivation and shape the behavior in a new, more productive direction.

Let's recap what I've taught you in these last two chapters. First, we looked at the four *negative* solutions to undesirable behavior. These are what I want you to stop doing.

- Eliminate the offender, by firing them, divorcing them or in some other way getting them out of your life.
- Extinguish the behavior by consistently failing to reinforce it.
- Negatively reinforce it by withdrawing support, or in some way disapproving of the behavior *as it is happening*.
- Punish the behavior in the hope that it will act as a deterrent.

Instead, I want you to substitute one of the four *positive* ways of changing other people's behavior that I taught you in this chapter:

1. Condition them to react with an incompatible behavior.
2. Put the undesirable behavior on cue.
3. Reinforce the lack of the undesirable behavior.
4. Remove the benefit for the undesirable behavior.

You are almost ready to start using these techniques. Move on to the next chapter right away, where you'll meet Dan Hill, the sales manager at Jenkins Pumps. Dan is frustrated with his career and ready to give up on his ambition to become a company president. You'll see how he uses all the techniques I've taught you to move his career into high gear.

Chapter Ten

9 Steps to a Self-Directed Life

I n this chapter I'm going to pull together all I've taught you about behavior shaping and turn it into a plan for success. To illustrate how it works let's look at Dan Hill, who's just turned forty and has an attractive wife Gayle, and two fine children. He graduated from State College with a business major and liberal arts minor. He stayed in college for another year, working hard on his MBA. Then he married Gayle and got a job in sales. At first, he kept going to college part time, to finish his MBA program. However, after a year the pressure of his work and his new family forced him to drop out. During his twenties, he held several selling jobs, but it wasn't until he joined his present company, Jenkins Pumps, that he had much success. Jenkins manufactures and sells submersible pumps that contractors use to pump out below ground construction sites. They're also used in mines, and in fountains and artificial waterfalls. His sales manager at Jenkins was the first to see real potential in Dan, and became his mentor. In Dan's third year with the pump company, he became their top salesperson. He was thirty-five when his mentor retired, and when the company chose Dan to take his place, he became the youngest sales manager in the company's seventy-two year history.

The next five years were the most exciting in his life. As he saw his two children move through grade school and into junior high, he dedicated himself to his career and worked harder than ever before. As the European Community started to take shape, he convinced the president of Jenkins Pumps of the potential for international sales. After a risky investment in buying a Dutch pump company, everything paid off for Dan when he made the biggest sale in the company's history, the pumps for the construction of the tunnel under the English Channel.

Since the euphoria of that sale, though, Dan's been depressed about his career. Jenkins Pumps is now one of 32 companies in the manufacturing group of a huge conglomerate. While he has a promising future as sales manager, he wonders if he'll ever be able to make the next step up the corporate ladder, to president of Jenkins or one of the other 31 companies in the group. Going to work doesn't excite him anymore, and he thinks frequently of quitting and starting his own company as a manufacturer's representative. He spends many hours thinking about how happy he was when he was an impoverished college student and took off for a semester to be a ski bum at Lake Tahoe.

Dan is in a typical mid-life slump. He fears that he'll never reach his youthful goal of becoming president of a Fortune 1000 company. He gets a great deal of joy from his marriage and his family, but he's not euphoric about it the way he was when he was twenty-five.

How can behavior shaping help Dan find success and happiness as the head of a corporation? Let's assume that Dan is a master at behavior shaping, and listen as we follow Dan through the nine steps to a self-directed life. Let's see if we can get him past his career doldrums and promoted to company president.

Step One—Select a Goal

Goals must be specific, attainable by your efforts, measurable, and have a time frame.

Dan's goal of becoming one of the 32 company presidents in his corporate manufacturing group is specific, so it passes the first test.

It's also attainable through his own efforts. If his goal was to become president of Jenkins, that wouldn't be so, because he'd be dependent on the current president dying, retiring or stepping down, and that may not happen. By broadening his goal to any one of the companies in the group, he probably won't fall into the trap of doing everything that he possibly could to be promoted, but wind up stymied because no opening occurs.

His goal is also measurable, so it passes the third test. By that, I mean that he'll know when he's reached it. That seems obvious, doesn't it? However, it would amaze you to know how many people make goals such as, "to be happy," "to be rich," or "to be fulfilled." Great objectives, but too vague. How are they ever going to know if they make it?

Dan's goal doesn't pass the fourth test, which is to have a time frame. If your goal doesn't have a time frame, you're daydreaming not goal setting. So, he must add a time frame. My advice is never set a goal longer than five years. You can do just about anything in five years.

So a good goal for Dan would be, "To become president of one of the companies in the manufacturing group within three years." That passes all four tests of a goal, because it's specific, attainable by his efforts, measurable, and has a time frame. Now he's ready to move to the next step.

Step Two—Determine the chain of events that must precede the successful result.

In this stage, Dan visualizes getting the promotion he wants and works back through the events he feels got him the job. It seems clear that to get what he wants, the president of Jenkins Pumps will have to push for his promotion with the head of the parent company manufacturing division. Yes, but what would cause him to want to do that?

Dan thinks about the AC/DC formula and tries to figure out if the president's driving life force is Acceptance, Competence, Direction or Control.

If he's an Acceptance driven person, he might not push for Dan's promotion if he thought that it would mean disagreeing with his boss, the vice-president of the manufacturing group. Dan might have to rely more on impressing the vice-president directly.

If he's a Competence driven person, the performance of his own company might concern him too much to let Dan go.

If he's a Control person, keeping his thumb on Dan may be more important than seeing Dan move up the corporate ladder.

Fortunately, Dan decides that he works for a man who is a Direction driven person. He has devoted his business life to the growth of the corporation. Dan feels that he can count on him to push for his promotion as long as he feels it's in the best interests of the corporation.

So, his president would certainly give a great deal of weight to Dan's performance as a sales manager. Then he would think, "Does Dan have the depth of management knowledge needed to run a company, or is his strength only in sales?" Finally, Dan's personal appearance and energy level might detract, because he's gained twenty pounds during the last three years.

Step Three—Establish a course.

Dan determines that he needs to improve in four areas to become the ideal candidate for a promotion:

1. His department's performance must be the best in the group, so he sets a target of a 50 percent increase without any drop in gross profit margins.

2. He needs to finish his MBA college program to round out his management expertise.

3. He must improve his health and appearance by losing twenty pounds, and raise his energy by getting on an exercise program.

Step Four. Establish target behaviors.

Then he determines his target behaviors. To meet his performance goal, what must he do? Note that I said *do,* not accomplish. The key is making a goal of the *behavior* that he must adopt to reach his goal.

In order to get the best out of his sales force, he decides that he must spend 15 days a month in the field, working with his sales people.

To get his MBA, he finds out that he'll have to dedicate two weekends a month for three years.

To lose the weight and get into shape, he plans a diet of fruit for breakfast, salad for lunch, and skipping his evening cocktails. For exercise, he sets a goal of running in 10K races a year from now.

Dan is wise enough to know that he must work into each of these new behavior patterns gradually. If he were suddenly to start working fifteen days a month in the field, spending two weekends a month taking classes, and running in 10 kilometer races, he knows that he'd never be able to sustain the pace. He would get discouraged quickly. So for each of these, he develops a graduated plan that eases him into his new target behavior.

He's presently spending five days a month in the field, so he plans to add one extra day a month. In ten months, he'll be at his target behavior.

To get his MBA he plans to take four units the first semester, and then add an additional four units each semester until he's carrying twelve units.

His exercise plan calls for him to walk a mile a day the first month, increase to two miles a day in the second month, and three miles a day in the third month. In the fourth month, he will start jogging.

Note that there's nothing in his plan about staying cheerful, or always thinking positively. The philosophy of behavior shaping says that thought follows behavior. First Dan must do the things that start moving him toward his goal. Then as soon as he starts seeing the results of his behavior, cheerful and positive thoughts will follow.

Step Five—Keep a journal.

Dan buys a blank exercise book, and starts keeping a journal. He takes it very seriously and thinks of it as notes for a book that he will write. To make it more fun, he even gives it a grandiose title: *Pathway to the Pres-*

idency. Every day he records his behavior—the things he does that bring him closer to his goal.

In the nineteenth century, many people kept detailed life-long journals. It was an expression of personal discipline. Ben Franklin found great value in this. He kept a weekly calendar chart that listed what he considered virtues. They included: temperance, letting others talk, keeping things in order, meeting goals, avoiding waste, being clean, staying calm and being industrious. Note that they're all behavioral goals—none of them are cognitive. He put an X each time he failed. He worked on one virtue at a time. Recent research confirms that journal keeping may be even more helpful in solving personal problems than sessions with a professional therapist.

Dan determines to make personal observation and record keeping a daily habit. He formulates a system that's easy and convenient. Every day he makes a note of what he did in his three target areas: improving the performance of his department, expanding his knowledge of management skills, and improving his health and appearance.

Dan finds that observing and recording his behavior this way is intriguing and very enlightening. It gives him the detached view of his behavior on the job that is much closer to the view that his boss has of him. Ben Franklin also found that what he was doing differed widely from what he thought he was doing. He said, "I was surprised to find myself so much fuller of faults than I had imagined, but I had the satisfaction of seeing them diminish."

Dan's purpose at this stage is to make detailed observations of his behavior in various situations, and he knows that the more precise his written records are, the more useful they will be. Soon, he will be able to see patterns emerging. For example, he finds that he has a tendency to spend time in the field with the top salespeople rather than the ones who really need his help. He also notices that he really applies himself in marketing classes that are relevant to his work as sales manager, but has to push himself to stay interested in classes that relate to the financial and operational side of management. Furthermore, he finds that he is most likely to find an excuse not to exercise when he's away from home, and learns to compensate for that.

At the top of the page he notes his estimate of the calories he's consumed that day, and if he drank any alcohol. As he becomes more interested in nutrition, he starts making note of the grams of fat, protein, and carbohydrates he consumes. He's fascinated to find out that he eats much more than he thought he did. He remembers reading a study that showed most people's self-observation to be very inaccurate. A researcher asked a group of people to write down from memory everything that they'd eaten in the previous week. Then the researcher put them on a diet that was the same as what they said they ate. All of them lost weight! So, Dan finds that the very act of writing down his behavior causes him to make beneficial changes.

For each target behavior Dan establishes a reinforcement. His passion is building a compact disc collection of classical music, so he decides to use that for reinforcement. For each day that he achieves his three target behavior goals—for nutrition, working with his sales force and studying for his MBA—he gives himself a check mark in his journal. When he has accumulated ten check marks, he rewards himself by buying another compact disc for his collection. He feels childish doing it, but he knows that it's a cornerstone to behavior shaping.

As Dan sees how behavior shaping is improving his performance, he starts using it on his sales force. When orders are backed up at the factory, he finds his salespeople spending too much time complaining about shipments. During calls intended to motivate those in the field to sell more, he ends up spending all the time listening to gripes about the factory. Soon they're using it as an excuse for poor performance. He decides to put the behavior on cue, which was positive solution number two in chapter nine. He sets up a weekly conference call with all his area sales managers during which they discuss any problems with shipment. He gets the head of the shipping department to join him on the call. During the call, they don't have to hold back and can be as vocal as they like in criticizing the factory. However, Dan won't listen to complaints about shipping during the rest of the week. If they bring it up, he quickly tells them to save it for the conference call.

He also uses behavior shaping on Mike Rader, who is one of his top salespeople but is a real prima donna. He produces over 10 million dollars in sales a year, but he's not a team player. Dan talks it over with some of the other sales managers in the manufacturing group, and most of them tell him that if Mike sells that much, Dan should let him act any way he wants. However, Dan thinks he can do better with behavior shaping. To turn Mike into a team player, he conditions him to react with an incompatible behavior, solution number one in chapter nine. Dan calls Mike and tells him that he wants him to make a presentation at their annual retreat in Vail the following July. He asks him to spend fifteen minutes a week on the phone with one of the other salespeople, learning about the problems they're having in the field and coming up with solutions. During the following months, whenever Dan talks to Mike, he has him give an update on his training assignment. At first, Dan wonders whether diverting Mike's attention from sales for even fifteen minutes a week might hurt his performance. However, soon he realizes that as Dan becomes more of a team player, his enthusiasm grows and his sales get even better. Also, he doesn't discount prices as much; because he wants to look good to the salespeople he's mentoring.

Step Six—Avoiding the pitfalls.

As Dan starts down the road to success, he is aware of the pitfalls that could stop him from going where he wants to go. The positive thinkers would criticize him for that, saying that any thought of failure could become a self-fulfilling prophecy. Dan just thinks it's smart. He wouldn't drive across the country without thinking what he would do if a fan belt broke or a tire blew out, so it makes sense to anticipate the difficulties he might run into on the road to success.

First, he wonders if he has enough willpower to make it. Fifteen days in the field with his sales force besides getting his MBA is a big commitment to make. He remembers a sermon that his minister gave once about temptation. He preached that to avoid sin, we must avoid the occasion for sin. If we want to avoid temptation, we should avoid things that tempt us. Don't sit in front of a large plate of food when you're on a diet. Don't be alone with the opposite sex if you want to be celibate. Dan thinks about how that applies to his will-power, and makes a new rule for himself: Don't make commitments or reconsider commitments when you're tired or discouraged. He knows that one of the problems he will have is canceling field trips at the last minute if something comes up at the office. So, he writes on the flyleaf of his journal, "If I ever feel that I can't stick with this plan, I will wait one week before modifying it in any way." Also, he determines to schedule visits with his salespeople at least two weeks ahead of time, making it harder for him to back out.

Dan knows enough about behavior shaping to know that a problem with willpower is really a problem with behavior and reinforcement. A behavior that is not reinforced will extinguish, and the reinforcement must be proportionate to the effort required to sustain the behavior. If you get discouraged to the point of giving up, it's probably because the effort you're asking of yourself is greater than the perceived reward. If it's unrealistic to increase the reward, then it's smart to reduce the effort by lowering the goal.

Dan remembers teaching this to a new salesperson who was scared to cold call. His goal was to speak to twenty new customers a day, but he found that the effort of overcoming his fear was so great that he couldn't do it. Dan got him on a program of reduced effort by changing his goal to placing twenty *calls* a day, even if he was only leaving a message with a secretary that he'd called. At the end of each day, the salesperson had to call Dan, who would then reinforce him for the twenty calls he'd made, even if he hadn't reached a single new customer. During the next month, Dan gradually raised the target behavior until the salesperson felt comfortable with the goal of speaking to twenty potential customers a day.

In another instance, Dan went even further than that. When the company assigned him a student as a summer intern, he found that cold calling terrified her so much; it scared her even to pick up the telephone. He lowered the target behavior to just dialing the telephone and hanging up before the other person answered. After reinforcing that behavior for two days, he raised the intern's target behavior to leaving a message. Dan knows that with behavior shaping, it's impossible to make your initial sub-goal too low, or your rate of advance too slow. The key is creating a chain of behavior that is reinforced at every stage, and then gradually building up to your target behavior.

The next pitfall that Dan considers is the danger of plateaus. He knows that when you're following a behavior modification program, you may make excellent progress for several weeks and then suddenly stop. You find that the next step in your program, although it's small and no more challenging than the previous steps, seems impossible to achieve. The easiest way to continue upward when you reach a plateau is to make the size of your next step even smaller than before. If that isn't possible, at least recognize that the plateau experience is common, and "ride it out" without setting any deadlines for yourself. If none of these techniques prove effective, it may be that what seemed to be a plateau is truly your upper limit. In that case, don't be afraid to re-evaluate your goal.

The third pitfall that Dan considers is cheating. Like plateaus, cheating is a common problem in behavior shaping. It means that even if you don't earn the reinforcement, you give it to yourself anyway. In Dan's case, this would mean buying a compact disc before he had earned it. If you find yourself "stealing" the reinforcer more than 10% of the time, you should lower your level of expectation to a more realistic level. Dan knows that if you're sticking to *any* schedule of reinforced behavior, you're moving in the right direction. Don't worry about your slow progress. Also, don't let short-term problems cause you to abandon your project. Instead, simply redesign it. Dan pledges to himself that he won't buy *any* compact disk unless he's earned the ten check marks that it takes to get the reinforcement. Even if he's in a music store in a distant town and finds a rare discontinued compact disc that he's drooling to own.

Step Seven—Study role models.

Dan knows that, just as he can learn from observing his own behavior, he can benefit from a detailed observation of someone who's already achieving the goal he wants for himself. Before he learned behavior shaping, he used to feel that imitative behavior was somehow distasteful or wrong, as if he were trying to be someone else instead of being himself. Then he realized that imitation is the basis for some of our most efficient learning experiences. Imitation is the way children learn complicated social behaviors as they're growing up. Dan has learned that he can shorten the learning curve of a new salesperson by three months, simply by having him spend a week in the field with a top performer. By observing good models, we can often perform detailed sequences of behavior accurately the first time we try. From observing someone else, we learn a general way of behaving throughout a chain of events. After adapting it to our style, we'll be acting in our own way and not anyone else's.

From the list of the 31 other sales managers in the manufacturing group, Dan picks six that he feels are on a fast track to promotion. At first, he's reluctant to approach them because he sees them as a potential competitor for the same promotion. Then he focuses again on his goal of becoming a top company president, and realizes that a big part of his success in that job will be in helping his sales managers do a better job. If nothing else he'll learn a great deal about how to help sales managers in other companies improve their performance. After talking to all six about their goals, he decides that two of them are so self-centered in their ambition that they wouldn't fit into a master-mind group. However, the other four are enthusiastic about pooling their knowledge and experiences, and agree to conference call once a week and meet every three months. Dan finds this one of the best career moves he has ever made. He not only learns a lot, but he finds that the joy of reporting to the group that he's been able to stay with his target behaviors is a powerful reinforcer.

Dan finds that getting advice from the other members of his master-mind group is invaluable. When you're observing chains of cause and effect in your own behavior, it's easy to get confused. He knows that discouragement is only a breakdown in the reinforcement of his behavior, but it's difficult sometimes to see the problem. There may be times when the effective behavioral response isn't obvious, or you're not able to recognize your own contribution to a dissatisfying chain of events. When that happens, he finds it invaluable to talk with someone who is successful at handling the situation.

Of course, Dan knows that you can also learn undesirable behavior patterns from role models. For example, since the role models for children are usually their mother and father, they often grow up with the same phobias as their parents. If a mother is afraid of snakes or thunderstorms, the child will probably develop the same undesirable behavior pattern. So, Dan pledges to imitate the most desirable traits of the members of his master-mind group, and quietly ignore their weak behavior patterns. "Imitate the best, ignore the rest," becomes his motto.

Step Eight—Visualize yourself accomplishing your behavioral goal.

Visualization was originally a cornerstone of cognitive psychology. It means to implant into the subconscious mind a powerful visual image of the desired result. The image then draws you to it, because it becomes a goal of the subconscious mind. Since Dan became a believer in behavior shaping, he has adapted the technique and uses it to build on his target behaviors. Instead of visualizing himself as president of a manufacturing group company, he visualizes his target behavior at the next level. For example, as he leaves the house for a two-mile walk, he imagines that he's leaving for a three-mile walk, something that is not his target behavior until the following month. He finds that when he does this, he always finishes his two mile walk feeling good, and thinking that he could have gone an extra mile. During the semester when he's taking four units, he visualizes himself as a person who normally takes eight units, and who for this semester has an unusually light study load. By doing this, he finds that he gets much less discouraged, and that he can easily move up to the next level of behavior when it's scheduled.

Step Nine—Re-evaluate your behavioral goals continuously.

On one hand, Dan knows the importance of writing down his goals and sticking with them. On the other hand, he has seen too many salespeople set ambitious goals and then get discouraged and quit when they weren't making them. Often, the person was doing the best they could. They had simply overestimated their potential, or economic conditions had changed and made the goal harder to reach. Since Dan learned about behavior shaping, he knows that it's more important to focus on the behavior, than to focus on the goal. He knows that if he is doing all the right things, the results will drop into place automatically.

He remembers a sales manager in his group who didn't make it, and was eventually replaced. Dan thought he was a talented hard working man, but that he spent too much time keeping track of where he was, and not enough time doing the things that would get him where he wanted to go. He had covered his office wall with charts and projections. His salespeople had to call him at least once a day to let him know how many calls they had made, how much they had sold, and to give him an updated prediction of the business they had coming on line. He meticulously tracked all of this on his wall charts. Dan thought it was great that he knew exactly where he stood on his goals, but felt that he would have been more successful if he spent less time focusing on his goals and more time concentrating on his behavior targets.

Dan believes that you must keep in mind that you and your environment are constantly changing. The best solution lies in continuing to ask yourself, "What is the behavior target I should be aiming for now?" and "Right now, what specific techniques should I use to hit that behavior target in the bull's-eye?"

Let's review now the nine steps to a self-directed life:

1. Select a goal. Be sure that it is specific, attainable by your efforts, measurable, and has a time frame.

2. Determine the chain of events that must precede the successful result. What must change in order for you to get where you want to go?

3. Establish a course. What behaviors must you change to get to your goal?

4. Establish target behaviors. Develop a plan that gradually steps you up to the level of behavior that you have targeted.

5. Keep a journal, because it enables you to see your behavior more objectively. Check off your successes and reinforce your behavior with rewards.

6. Avoid the pitfalls. Understand that loss of willpower is really a problem with behavior and reinforcement. Look out for plateaus and the temptation to cheat by giving yourself reinforcement even if you haven't earned it.

7. Study role models, preferably by setting up a master-mind group. Remember to imitate the best, and ignore the rest.

8. Visualize yourself accomplishing your behavioral goal, which is far more powerful than merely visualizing the result.

9. Re-evaluate your behavioral goals continuously. The key to behavior shaping is to reinforce constantly the desired behavior. If you're having trouble reaching a target behavior, you should lower the goal, and keep on reinforcing. As soon as you feel that you're no longer stretching to reach your target behavior, because it has become too easy, raise your behavior target again.

Dan put his program into effect and used what he had learned about behavior shaping to keep himself and his sales force on track. He saw his performance improve gradually and in the third year of his plan he attained a 56 percent increase in sales, with a 6 percent increase in gross profit. He finished his MBA program with a 3.1 grade point average, and was able to get his weight down 25 pounds, so that even when he put back on 5 pounds, he was still able to maintain his target weight. His wife Gayle says he looks better now that he did when they married.

One day his president stopped by his office and handed him a folder of airplane tickets. With a strange smile on his face, he said, "Dan, I know you value your weekends with your family, but I'd like you to fly to

New York this Sunday. You have an appointment at corporate headquarters at ten o'clock Monday morning. Here are your first class tickets, and a reservation for a suite at the Plaza Hotel. I'd suggest you be sitting outside the CEO's office at least fifteen minutes early."

"Does that mean it's happening?" Dan asked.

"I can't tell you a thing more than I have. But I will tell you this. I think you've done wonders for this company in the last three years. I can't believe how you've become so focused and how you've been able to bring the sales force together so well. The parent company has come a long way, but it has an even greater future, and we need high achievers like you to keep us moving forward." And then, with a rare show of emotions he came around the desk, hugged Dan, and whispered, "Good luck, son."

The following Monday morning he was shown into the boardroom at corporate headquarters. Around the long conference table sat all the top corporate executives. The CEO took the time to introduce him to everyone individually as if he was the newest member of the most exclusive country club on the planet. When they were down to business and Dan found out what they had in mind for him, it stunned him. It would have thrilled him to get the presidency of any one of the thirty-two companies in the group. What they gave him was the presidency of Hunter Tools, the second largest company in the group, with worldwide sales of almost 3 billion dollars. As the VP of operations went over his compensation package, Dan's head was spinning. He thought of how only three years ago, he was depressed over his career and wondering whether he should drop out. Now he was on top of the world, and earning more money that he ever dreamed of making.

Finally the CEO said, "Dan, we've jumped you over half a dozen good people to give you a shot at Hunter Tools. But you earned it with your outstanding performance during the last three years. I know you won't let us down. For the next couple of years, you're going to be working harder than you ever thought possible until you get on top of the opportunities there. So first, we'd like you to take some time off. We want you to spend the rest of the week in Manhattan enjoying yourself. Everything at our expense of course. My secretary will give you a package of tickets to all the top shows and a generous voucher so that you can do some shopping for new clothes to match your new position. So, have fun. Friday night the chairman is expecting you at his town house for a dinner party to celebrate."

Dan hesitated, "That all sounds wonderful, sir, but I'd really like to get back and share all this good news with my family."

"We thought you might say that, so we flew them in so they could spend the week with you." The conference room doors flew open and his wife and children were running toward him. As they walked out into the bright sunlight of Fifth Avenue, tears of joy ran down all of their faces.

The following Sunday they were having lunch at the famous Rainbow Room restaurant at the top of Rockefeller Center. Over Long Island, they could see a flock of Canadian Geese flying south for the winter. "Keep flying," said Dan, "just keep flying. Don't ever, ever give up."

CPSIA information can be obtained
at www.ICGtesting.com
Printed in the USA
BVHW042017270119
538781BV00006B/29/P

9 781722 500276